COUNTRIES OF THE WORLD

Czech Republic

Gareth Stevens Publishing
A WORLD ALMANAC EDUCATION GROUP COMPANY

About the Author: Lindy Roux is South African by birth, but she and her husband have lived in various countries in Europe, Africa, and Asia. They now reside in Atlanta, Georgia, in the United States with their three daughters. The family still enjoys traveling and learning about different cultures.

Written by
LINDY ROUX

Edited by
LYNELLE SEOW

Edited in the U.S. by
**CATHERINE GARDNER
ALAN WACHTEL**

Designed by
GEOSLYN LIM

Picture research by
SUSAN JANE MANUEL

First published in North America in 2004 by
Gareth Stevens Publishing
A World Almanac Education Group Company
330 West Olive Street, Suite 100
Milwaukee, Wisconsin 53212 USA

Please visit our web site at
www.garethstevens.com
For a free color catalog describing
Gareth Stevens Publishing's list of high-quality
books and multimedia programs,
call 1-800-542-2595 (USA) or 1-800-387-3178 (Canada).
Gareth Stevens Publishing's fax: (414) 332-3567.

© **TIMES MEDIA PRIVATE LIMITED 2004**
Originated and designed by
Times Editions
An imprint of Times Media Private Limited
A member of the Times Publishing Group
Times Centre, 1 New Industrial Road
Singapore 536196
http://www.timesone.com.sg/te

Library of Congress Cataloging-in-Publication Data
Roux, Lindy.
Czech Republic/ by Lindy Roux.
p. cm – (Countries of the world)
Summary: Provides an overview of the geography, history, government, people, arts, foods, and other aspects of life in the Czech Republic.
Includes bibliographical references and index.
ISBN 0-8368-3109-8 (lib. bdg.)
1. Czech Republic—Juvenile literature. [1. Czech Republic.]
I. Title. II. Countries of the world (Milwaukee, Wis.)
DB2011.R68   2004
943.71—dc22   2003060724

Printed in Singapore

1 2 3 4 5 6 7 8 9 08 07 06 05 04

Contents

AN OVERVIEW OF THE CZECH REPUBLIC

Although the Czech Republic, founded in 1993, is one of the world's youngest countries, its culture and identity go back centuries. Known to its people as Ceská Republika, the Czech Republic is a small country in the heart of Europe that consists of two major regions, Bohemia and Moravia.

The republic's history is marked by periods of occupation and control by the Hapsburg dynasty, Nazi Germany, and the Soviet Union. This caused the Czech people to slowly forge the strong national identity often seen in Czech protest art, literature, and music. Today, the Czech Republic is a free and independent country and has made great strides toward becoming an important part of the international community.

Opposite: **Fish farms operating in the country's many man-made lakes breed freshwater carp and trout.**

Below: **Prague Castle sits imposingly on a hill overlooking the city of Prague and the Vltava River. The spires of St. Vitus's Cathedral tower above the rooftops.**

THE FLAG OF THE CZECH REPUBLIC

Gaining independence in 1993, the Czech Republic adopted the same flag that had been used by Czechoslovakia since 1920 — a blue equilateral triangle with its base at the hoist side and two horizontal bands, the top white and the bottom red. The red and white symbolize the old Bohemian coat of arms; white represents Bohemia and red represents Moravia. Blue used to represent Slovakia. Since independence, blue became the symbol of the country's sovereignty. The flag was changed briefly during the Nazi occupation to three horizontal bands of white, red, and blue. The Slovakian flag shares the same colors as the flag of the Czech Republic.

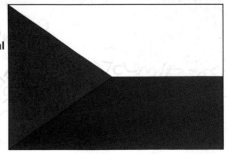

Geography

In Shakespeare's *Winter's Tale,* a character talks of the coasts of Bohemia. In reality, Bohemia — part of the Czech Republic — has no coastline. The whole country is landlocked, sharing borders with Germany, Austria, Slovakia, and Poland. The country covers about 30,400 square miles (78,740 square kilometers).

Mountains

The landscape of the Czech Republic is varied. The region of Bohemia, located in the western part of the country, consists of low mountains surrounding hills, plains, and plateaus. Moravia, on the other hand, is very hilly.

The Bohemian-Moravian Highlands separate Bohemia and Moravia. The Ore Mountains and the Krkonoše Mountains are found respectively on the country's borders with Germany and Poland. The Krkonoše range includes Mount Sněžka, the highest point in the Czech Republic, at 5,256 feet (1,602 meters).

The Little Carpathians, the Javorníky Mountains, and the Jeseníky Mountains surround Moravia. Farther south of the Jeseníky Mountains is an area of limestone known as the

Below: **Moravia is primarily an agricultural region.**

6

Moravian Karst, where water erosion has formed underground caves, streams, and rock formations. There are over 2,000 karst caves around the country.

Rivers and Lakes

The Czech Republic is extensively crossed by its three major river systems — the Labe (Elbe), the Odra (Oder), and the Morava. The Vltava River, a tributary of the Labe, is the republic's longest river and passes through its capital, Prague. The Labe eventually drains into the North Sea. The Morava River flows through Moravia and empties into the Danube River, which, in turn, finds its way to the Black Sea. The Odra flows north to Poland and eventually into the Baltic Sea.

Most of the Czech Republic's lakes have been artificially created for fish farming. The country has about 21,800 man-made lakes covering more than 101,000 acres (41,000 hectares).

The Czech Republic has many mineral water springs that are said to have healing qualities. Spa towns, such as Karlovy Vary, are well-known for their thermal springs. The radioactive spring in Jáchymov is said to be good for the nervous system.

Above: **Numerous bridges cut across the Vltava River. The most famous bridge is Charles Bridge (*second bridge from the front*), which is lined with many statues of Czech historical figures.**

THE ANGRY VLTAVA

The Vltava is a scenic and calm waterway. It is used for canoeing, boating, and fishing during the summer. On some occasions, the river turns violent. Disasters occur when the river overflows with raging waters, flooding the cities and towns along its banks.

(A Closer Look, page 46)

Four Seasons

Because of its diverse landscape, the Czech Republic experiences variable climates and precipitation levels, both of which also depend on altitude. The interior plateau areas enjoy a temperate climate with warm summers and cold winters, while the mountainous areas endure harsher winters and receive heavier rainfall. The southern areas of Bohemia have hot summers and milder winters. Across the country, the average temperature in summer is about 68° Fahrenheit (20° Celsius). The hottest month is July. In winter, temperatures drop to an average of 23° F (-5° C), and the average temperature ranges between 12° F (-11° C) and 32° F (0° C).Winter conditions in the mountains are harsher.

Precipitation falls throughout the year in the Czech Republic. The lowlands receive an average of 18 to 30 inches (45 to 76 cm), and the mountains receive an average of 60 inches (152 cm) or more. Summers are characterized by periods of warm, dry weather broken by sporadic rain or thunderstorms, during which flooding can occur. In winter, days are cloudy and cold. Winter fog often hangs over the lowlands, making winters humid.

Above: **A Czech boy plays in fallen autumn leaves. The Czech Republic experiences four seasons.**

Plants and Animals

Forests still cover about one-third of the Czech Republic, in spite of widespread deforestation for cultivation. Spruce, beech, and oak trees make up the higher mountainside forests. Grass and lichen can be found at higher altitudes. Mixed forests of ash and maple grow in the valleys.

The Czech Republic is rich in fauna. Animals that are common to the mountainous areas include wolves, brown bears, wild boar, lynxes and other wildcats, chamois, foxes, marmots, otters, marten, mink, and the endangered mouflon. The lowlands are home to hares and badgers. Communities of pheasants, ducks, wild geese, and other game birds can be found in woodlands and marshes. Other birds, such as eagles, vultures, and owls, also inhabit the forests.

National parks have been set up to protect the country's diverse flora and fauna. The Bohemian Forest and the Krkonoše National Park have been protected areas since the 1960s. The Šumava National Park and the Podyjí National Park are also protected nature reserves. The Krkonoše National Park is the largest national park in the country. The Czech Republic has had four national parks since the establishment of the Bohemian Switzerland National Park in 2000.

THE SUREFOOTED CHAMOIS

Found along the slopes of Czech mountains is the chamois (*above*), a timid animal seldom seen by people. It jumps from rock to rock without falling or slipping. Most people know the animal for its famous skin.
(*A Closer Look, page 66*)

Left: The marten is a small, slender-bodied carnivore. Its fur is soft and thick.

History

The earliest known inhabitants of the land were Celtic people called the Boii, from whom Bohemia derived its name. In about the fifth century A.D., Slavic tribes settled in the regions of Bohemia, Moravia, and Silesia. By the ninth century, the Slavic tribes united and formed the Great Moravian Empire, under which Christianity was introduced to the people of the Cechove tribe, from which Czechs derive their name. The Přemysl dynasty came to power in the tenth century and formed the Bohemian Kingdom. This dynasty unified warring Czech tribes and ruled Bohemia and Moravia from the tenth century until 1306. In the fourteenth century, political and artistic accomplishment in the Bohemian Kingdom reached new heights under Charles V, who was the Bohemian king and Holy Roman Emperor. Charles IV made Prague the capital of the kingdom, and the city became a center for learning.

THE PRINCESS-NUN

In the Přemysl dynasty was born a princess who sacrificed her wealth and her title to care for and feed the poor. She became known for her great devotion to her faith and has been recognized as a saint. *(A Closer Look, page 64)*

Left: **Charles University in Prague was founded in 1348 and is named after Charles IV.**

Left: **In 1618, two Catholic officials were thrown out a window of Prague Castle, in an event known as the second Defenestration. "Defenestration" means to throw someone or something out a window. A first defenestration occurred about two centuries earlier, when several councilors were thrown out of a town hall window and killed by a group of Hussites.**

Centuries of Conflict

In 1415, a religious reformer, Jan Hus, was burned at the stake for heresy. His death marked the beginning of decades of religious conflict between Catholics and the group of reformers known as the Hussites. The Hussites, led by Jan Žižka, called for changes in church practices, threatened the German Catholic dominance of Europe, and consequently revived Czech nationalism. Calm returned to the country when an agreement was reached between Hussite Bohemia and the Catholic Church.

In 1526, Ferdinand I, a member of the Austrian Catholic Hapsburg dynasty, ascended the Bohemian throne. This was the beginning of more than three centuries of Hapsburg power that saw struggles both between the monarchy and the Czech people and between Catholics and Protestants. In the early seventeenth century, an all-out clash erupted after two Catholic officials were thrown out of one of the windows of Prague Castle. The conflict escalated into the Thirty Years' War (1618–1648). In 1620, the Czechs were finally defeated in the infamous Battle of White Mountain. Their defeat secured the ruling Hapsburg empire, which eventually led to the catholicizing of the nation, the loss of the Czech nobility, and the suppression of Czech culture. German later became the official language.

The Czech people would not taste freedom until the collapse of the Austrian-Hungarian Empire at the end of World War I 300 years later.

Czechoslovakia

In October 1918, the state of Czechoslovakia was formed, marking a union between the Czech lands and Slovakia that would last seventy-five years. The new republic had three regions — Moravia, Bohemia, and Slovakia. Tomáš Garrigue Masaryk became its first president. This period, known as The First Republic, was characterized by flourishing arts, literature, industry, and trade. Czechoslovakia became one of the world's ten most developed nations.

In 1939, the country was occupied by German Nazi troops under Adolf Hitler's direction. Civilians were forced to work in factories supplying arms to the German military. Nazi opponents, as well as Czech Roma and Czech Jews, were arrested and sent to concentration camps, where many of them died. In 1942, Hitler ordered the complete destruction of the Czech villages of Lidice and Ležáky in retaliation for the assassination of the German governor of Czechoslovakia. Oppression under Nazi Germany continued until 1945, when Germany was defeated by the Allies.

THE CHILDREN OF TEREZÍN

The Holocaust was a terrible time for the Jews throughout Europe. Even children, including those imprisoned in the town of Terezín, could not escape extermination. Few lived to tell of their experiences. Most can only be known through the drawings and poems they left behind.
(A Closer Look, page 50)

Below: Hitler is saluted by the Sudeten Germans, a minority group that lived in Czechoslovakia. Most Czechs scorned the Nazi presence.

From Communism to the Velvet Revolution

In 1945, the country's boundaries were restored, and the previous government was reinstated. The Communist Party, however, gained dominance in the 1946 national elections, and in 1948, after a coup d'etat, Czechoslovakia became a communist country. During the early part of 1968, the country enjoyed a period of liberalization under Alexander Dubček. Dubček's vision was for "socialism with a human face," reflecting popular support for democracy and an end to censorship. This short period, known as the Prague Spring, was later crushed by the 1968 Soviet invasion. The 1970s and 1980s marked a period known as "normalization," during which the Czechoslovak economy came to a stand still, and persecution and repression became part of daily life.

On January 1, 1977, more than 250 human rights activists signed a manifesto that became known as Charter 77. The document criticized the Czechoslovak government for not observing the human rights commitment it made in official documents and as stated in the Czech constitution. In 1989, the Velvet Revolution brought more than forty years of Soviet control to an end using no violence. A group called the Civic Forum led the country's return to democracy. One of the Civic Forum's leaders was the dissident Václav Havel, who became Czechoslovakia's first postcommunist president.

The Velvet Divorce and Independence

Between 1991 and 1993, a wave of Slovak nationalism swept over Czechoslovakia. On January 1, 1993, Czechoslovakia was dissolved, and two independent nations — the Czech Republic and Slovakia — were born. This separation became known as the "Velvet Divorce." Václav Havel had some difficulty accepting the division and stepped down as president of Czechoslovakia. He was elected president of the Czech Republic later in 1993.

Since its independence, the Czech Republic has become a member of the North Atlantic Treaty Organization (NATO), the Organization for Economic Cooperation and Development (OECD), and the Central European Free Trade Agreement (CEFTA). The country's application to become part of the European Union (EU) was accepted in 2002, and formal accession to the EU is planned for 2004. The Czech Republic is also a member of the World Trade Organization (WTO), the International Monetary Fund, the World Bank, and the European Bank for Reconstruction and Development.

In February 2003, after thirteen years of presidency, Václav Havel stepped down as the Czech Republic's president. Former prime minister, Václav Klaus, was elected as his successor.

VÁCLAV HAVEL— PLAYWRIGHT TO PRESIDENT.

Václav Havel started his career in the arts. Swept into the political limelight because of his deep convictions on human rights and democracy, he left a lasting legacy, not only for his long presidency, but for leading the Czech Republic into the international arena.
(A Closer Look, page 72)

Left: Václav Havel (*right*) shakes hands with his successor, Václav Klaus (*left*), at a dinner party at Prague Castle after Klaus was sworn in as president of the Czech Republic.

Jan Hus (c.1369–1415)

After Jan Hus earned his master's degree in 1396, he was ordained as a priest, and he became interested in the works of British reformer John Wyclif. Hus denounced certain practices within the Catholic Church that he felt went against the scriptures. In 1412, he left Prague and went into exile for two years. While in exile, he wrote *De Ecclesiâ*, a work highly critical of the state of the Church. In 1415, he was invited to the Council of Constance under the pretext of a hearing with the Pope. There, he was captured, tried, convicted as a heretic, and burned at the stake.

Maria Theresa

Maria Theresa (1717–1780)

Maria Theresa became the empress of the Hapsburg lands in 1740, after a change in the law introduced by her father allowed a female to take the throne if there were no direct male descendents. She ruled as empress for only two months before a war broke out, and she was no longer recognized as empress. After the war, her husband, Francis I, became the emperor. Maria Theresa opposed the rights of the Catholic nobility and introduced reforms to reduce widespread social oppression.

František Palacký (1798–1876)

František Palacký was a major figure of the Czech revival in the mid-nineteenth century and is regarded as the father of the modern Czech nation. He wrote a five-volume *History of the Czech People* on the nation's struggle for political freedom. Palacký's work inspired further awareness of Czech culture and influenced later leaders, such as Tomáš Garrigue Masaryk.

František Palacký

Alexander Dubček (1921–1992)

Alexander Dubček is best known for instituting radical reforms in communist-run Czechoslovakia. Dubček's liberal policies alarmed the Soviet leadership and resulted in the Soviet invasion of Czechoslovakia in August 1968. In 1970, he was expelled from the Communist Party, sent to Slovakia, and forced to work as a forestry official. After the collapse of the communist government in November 1989, Dubček was elected chairman of the Federal Assembly.

Alexander Dubček

Government
and the Economy

Government

The Czech Republic is a parliamentary democracy with three branches — executive, legislative, and judicial. The executive branch consists of the president, the prime minister, and the cabinet. The legislative branch — or Parliament — is made up of the Chamber of Deputies (200 members) and the Senate (81 members). The Chamber of Deputies is the country's main legislative body. The judicial branch includes the Supreme Court and the Constitutional Court.

The Czech president is elected by Parliament and serves a five-year term. The president appoints the prime minister and the cabinet. Václav Klaus was elected president of the Czech Republic in March 2003. His prime minister is Dr. Vladimír Špidla, and the four deputy prime ministers are Stanislav Gross, Cyril Svoboda, Pavel Rychetský, and Petr Mareš.

Senate members serve six-year terms. One-third of the Senate is elected every two years. In contrast, members of the Chamber of Deputies serve four-year terms. Unlike the Senate,

NOT JUST ANY CASTLE

Like the Bohemian princes of the past, the Czech government can lay claim to having its offices in a historic seat of governance — Prague Castle. More than a building or office, it is a monument to Czech history and architecture. *(A Closer Look, page 62)*

Left: **Czech Prime Minister Vladimír Špidla (*far left*) listens to Communist deputy Vojtěch Filip (*far right*) in a parliament session on the deployment of Czech soldiers to Iraq.**

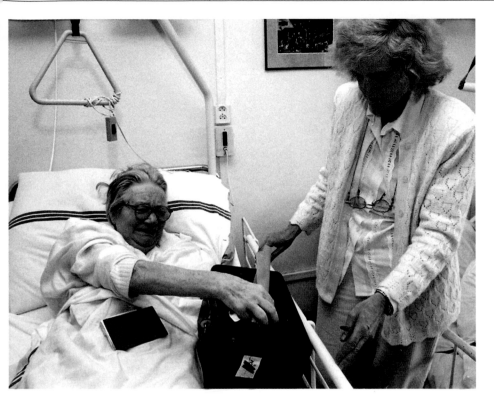

Left: An 81-year-old woman casts her vote into a portable ballot box during the country's general elections in 1998. Universal suffrage, which means that everyone has a right to vote once they are eighteen years old, is practiced in the Czech Republic.

the Chamber of Deputies can be dissolved during a term, which results in an early election for the following term. The president appoints the chairman and officers of the Supreme Court for unlimited terms and also appoints the chairman and deputy chairmen of the Constitutional Court for fixed 10-year terms.

For administrative purposes, the country is divided into thirteen administrative regions, called *kraje* (KHRA-ay), and the capital, Prague.

The Czech Republic's constitution became effective on January 1, 1993. It emphasizes respect for human rights and freedoms, and it states that the people are the source of all power in the state. They exercise their power through legislative, executive, and judicial representatives.

Political Parties

Political parties currently represented in Parliament include the Czech Social Democratic Party (CSSD), the Civic Democratic Party (ODS), the Communist Party of Bohemia and Moravia (KSCM), the Christian Democratic Union-Czechoslovak Peoples Party (KDU-CSL), and the Freedom Union (US). Political parties are free to compete for representation in Parliament.

Economy

The Czech Republic's highly skilled labor force, developed infrastructure, and relatively rapid adaptation to democracy has earned the country a reputation as one of the most economically and politically stable postcommunist countries.

After the fall of communism in 1989, the country moved from a centrally planned economy to a free market economy. Many former state enterprises were privatized, and foreign investment led to strong economic growth. In 1999, the Czech Republic was one of Europe's best examples of a free market economy. The country's growing budget deficit, however, remains a cause for concern.

The Czech Republic's natural resources include anthracite, bituminous, and brown coals, which are burned to provide energy for the country. Over half the country's energy needs are met by coal. Coal use has, however, wreaked havoc on the country's environment. Nuclear energy is increasing in importance as the country works to reduce its dependence on coal and safeguard its environment from further damage.

The Czech Republic's service sector provides 56 percent of the country's gross domestic product (GDP) and 60 percent of its total employment. Manufacturing, the country's second-largest sector, accounts for 41 percent of the country's GDP and employs

ACID RAIN

The country's heavy reliance on coal to fuel its industries and factories has led to widespread damage of large areas of natural forests. Pollution in the form of acid rain is a serious threat to the country's environment.

(*A Closer Look*, page 44)

35 percent of its workforce. The country makes automobiles, machine tools, and machinery, as well as chemicals, iron, steel, textiles, and glass.

Agriculture, which employs about 5 percent of the workforce, is the Czech economy's smallest sector. Crops such as corn, sugar beets, potatoes, wheat, hops, barley, and rye, as well as livestock such as hogs, cattle, sheep, and poultry are the most significant products for both domestic consumption and for export. Food-processing, including the making of the famous Czech beers, has also become a lucrative export industry.

In recent years, international trade has become increasingly important, especially with other European Union (EU) countries. The Czech Republic's largest trading partner is neighboring Germany. Important imports and exports include machinery, transport equipment, chemicals, raw materials, and fuel.

As the country formally prepares to enter the EU in 2004, its government is working hard to encourage greater economic transformation in order to align the country with EU market regulations and policies. The EU, in turn, is helping the Czech Republic develop its economy by providing financial assistance and investing in the development of the country's infrastructure.

BOHEMIAN CRYSTAL AND GLASS

Bohemian crystal is sold throughout the world. With a history going back centuries, the glass and crystal industry is not new to the country. It is no wonder that the Czechs are among the leading players in this business, having had centuries to hone this craft into an art.
(A Closer Look, page 48)

Left: Škoda cars are produced in the Czech Republic. The Škoda company has several automobile plants operating in the country and employs more than 24,000 Czech workers.

People and Lifestyle

In 2002, the Czech Republic had a population of about 10.3 million, and the population growth rate was estimated at -0.07 percent. A negative population growth rate means that there are more deaths than births in the country. The ethnic composition of the country is dominated by Bohemians, who represent 81 percent of the population. Thirteen percent are Moravians and 3 percent are ethnic Slovaks who stayed in the country after the 1993 division. Germans, Roma, Poles, and Silesians make up the remaining 3 percent of the population. The Czech Republic also has a growing Vietnamese community.

Forty years of communism produced a society with little distinction between social classes, and few class divisions exists in the Czech Republic today. Most Czechs consider themselves egalitarian. Status in Czech society comes from knowledge, ability, and education. Despite little class distinction, Czech society can be intolerant, in particular against the Roma minority. The strong Czech national identity and pride, while resulting in a strong sense of community among many Czech people, contributes to this prejudice.

Below: **Couples dance in a park in the summer for leisure as well as for exercise. The Czech life expectancy has increased. Czechs born today are estimated to live about 5 years longer than Czechs born in the 1970s.**

Czech Roma

The Czech Republic is home to between 150,000 and 300,000 Roma. The Roma, thought to originate from India, arrived in central Europe in the fifteenth century. Because they passed through Bohemia and on to France, the term "Bohemians" became synonymous with "gypsies," as the Roma are also called. Throughout history, the Roma have experienced discrimination not only socially, but also in education, employment, housing, and health care. Roma unemployment rates are seven times that of the Czech national average. Some preventive measures have been adopted, but social discrimination remains. Opinion polls in the 1990s showed that many Czechs favored separating the Roma from the rest of Czech society or, if possible, removing them from the country. As a result of these attitudes, many Czech Roma are still victims of violent hate crimes. The issue of racism against the Roma became more prominent because of the Czech Republic's joining the EU. The country's policies toward the human rights of the Roma are under scrutiny by the EU.

Family Life

About 70 percent of Czechs live in apartments in large cities. Because housing is limited and expensive, many adult children live with their parents after marriage until they can find apartments of their own. It is not uncommon for the grandmother in a family to take care of her grandchildren when their parents go to work. The grandmother, or *babička* (BAHB-ish-ka), is an important part of the Czech family. She is regarded with great respect and love. The 1855 novel *Babička*, a Czech classic by Božena Němcová, immortalized the role of the grandmother in Czech culture.

Czech Women

Women in the Czech Republic traditionally add the suffix "-ová" to their last names. The gesture traditionally indicates that they belonged to either their fathers or husbands. For example, a Czech man may have the last name of Novák, while his wife's last name will be Nováková. With an increasing number of marriages between Czechs and non-Czechs, a new law was passed in 2001 allowing some women to drop the suffix from their last names.

Czech women represent about half of the country's labor force, and most of them work full-time outside the home. They are equal to men in the eyes of the law, but women still earn an average of 25 percent less than their male counterparts for the same job. The income gap, however, is narrowing. Many Czech women also accept the responsibilities of keeping house and raising children along with having careers.

Marriage

Traditionally, Czechs married young, especially those living in rural areas. Young men often married in their early twenties. Young people in the cities today, however, are following international trends and are marrying later. In 1991, the average marrying age was twenty-five for men and twenty-two for women. In 2001, the marrying age rose to twenty-nine for men and twenty-seven for women. People are marrying later partly because it is becoming more expensive to start a family. For their marriage ceremonies, some Czechs choose to have traditional village weddings, which are characterized by singing, dancing, and elaborate meals. The wedding couple and their guests wear traditional costumes with elaborate embroidery.

Below: According to tradition, a Czech groom must saw a piece of wood during the wedding celebration.

Education

The Czech Republic has a literacy rate of nearly 100 percent. Education is considered to be very important, and those with academic titles are highly respected. The Czech school year runs from September to the end of June followed by a two-month vacation for the summer in July and August.

Children begin school at age six and attend for nine years. Basic (or elementary) school has two stages — years one to five and years six to nine. Czech students study subjects such as Czech language and literature, foreign languages, physics, biology, civics, chemistry, geography, mathematics, and history. Art and music are also part of the curriculum. At the end of basic school, students earn the *Vysvědčeni* (VEES-vehd-cheh-nee) diploma. Education is provided free of charge, and most schools are state-run.

Students need to pass entrance examinations to enter the secondary school of their choice. Secondary education is offered at three main types of schools: gymnasiums, technical schools,

Below: **Boys and girls are given equal opportunities for education. Parents can choose to send their children to public schools, private schools, or parochial schools. Teachers usually teach in the Czech language, but some schools use English or German.**

Left: Two students surf the Internet at the Czech University of Technology, which dates to 1717. It was the first of its kind in Central Europe.

and vocational schools. Gymnasiums provide general education to prepare students for higher education. Technical schools and vocational schools prepare students for various professions.

After secondary education, students can enter universities . The Czech Republic has twenty-three universities. Most Czech universities have strict entrance requirements. Charles University in Prague is the oldest university in central Europe and the most prestigious university in the country. An increasing number of foreign students are enrolling in Czech universities. The vast majority are from Slovakia, Greece, the United Kingdom, Russia, and Ukraine.

Shortly after the fall of the communist regime in 1989, many English language schools were established. Since most people only spoke Czech and Russian, these schools became popular. Today, learning English is considered a critical skill, especially after the county's entry into the EU. English is seen as a means to communicate with the rest of Europe, and knowing English opens up more job opportunities for Czechs.

The Czech educational system is being refined. Greater autonomy will be given to individual schools to improve their academic programs to provide better quality education.

Religions

Christianity was brought to Bohemia in the ninth century by two missionary brothers, Cyril and Methodius. After the tenth century, when the Bohemian Kingdom came under the control of the Holy Roman Empire, Roman Catholicism became widespread for the next three centuries. The execution of religious reformer Jan Hus fueled the conflict between Roman Catholics and the Protestant reformers who objected to some Catholic practices. The Catholic Hapsburg empire tried to extend the reach of the Catholic Church and to stop the growing Czech Protestant culture. Under Soviet control, all forms of religion were restricted.

Freedom to Worship — or Not To

Religious freedom was reestablished in the Czech Republic after the Velvet Revolution in 1989. Restrictions enforced by the communist regime were removed, and churches were once more able to operate freely. Many Czechs, however, do not believe in any religion. As of 2002, about 40 percent of Czechs declared themselves atheists.

Above: **Catholic priests celebrate a Mass outdoors on a pleasant Sunday morning. Roman Catholicism has remained the most popular religion in the country.**

Nevertheless, the dominance of churches and cathedrals in the skylines of most of the country's major cities testifies to the long history of Christianity and, particularly, Roman Catholicism in the Czech Republic. Thirty-nine percent of Czechs are Roman Catholics. Many more adhere to the Catholic traditions of their upbringing and participate in the Catholic observances, such as Lent and Easter, celebrated throughout the year.

Since the Reformation movement in the sixteenth century, the Protestant Church has played an important role in the Czech Republic. Today, 5 percent of Czechs attend Protestant churches, including the Moravian Church, the Church of the Czechs, and the Hussite Church.

Thirteen percent of Czechs claim religions other than Christianity, including Judaism. Before the Nazi occupation, there were almost 360,000 Czechoslovak Jews. Most were killed in the Holocaust. Today, the Czech Jewish community numbers just a few thousand. The names of 80,000 Jews who died during one of the largest pogroms in Prague are written on the walls of Prague's Pinkas Synagogue. Prague has the country's largest Jewish community.

Below: **The Jewish cemetery in Prague is a reminder of the fate of Czech Jews during the Holocaust.**

27

Language and Literature

Like Slovak and Polish, Czech is a western Slavic language. It contains German and Latin influences, as well as the influence of Old Church Slavonic, the language devised by the missionary brothers Cyril and Methodius and used to translate the Bible. The language is also loosely related to the eastern and southern Slavic dialects, including Russian and Bulgarian

The earliest written forms of the Czech language used Slavic characters, but these were later replaced by the Roman alphabet. In the fifteenth century, the religious reformer Jan Hus devised a script unique to the Czech language by placing diacritical marks over Roman letters to indicate Czech pronunciations and sounds. Hus's system is still used today.

Czech was one of the two official languages of the former Czechoslovakia, and it became the official language of the Czech Republic after the Velvet Divorce.

Below: **Posters on a wall advertise cultural events in Prague. The majority of the country's population speaks Czech as a first language, while Slovak is the first language of the country's largest minority group. Hungarian, Polish, German, Ukrainian, Romany, and Russian are among the other languages spoken in the republic.**

Left: Czech-born writer Milan Kundera (*right*) is famous for his books *The Unbearable Lightness of Being* (1984) and *Immortality* (1990). In 1975, Kundera and his wife (*left*) emigrated to France.

Czech Literature

Czech literature dates back to the fourteenth century. During the Hapsburg reign, the Czech language lost its prominence and influence. In 1918, after independence, Czech literature began to flourish again. Over time, the Czech Republic has been home to some of the world's most celebrated writers and thinkers. Jan Ámos Komenský, also known as Comenius, is among the most famous Czech literary figures. He wrote about how society can be improved through education. His works have steered the development of Czech intellectual culture. In the Czech Republic, school children refer to him as "the teacher of nations."

Czech writer Karel Čapek coined the word "robot" in his 1921 play *Rossum's Universal Robots*, or *R.U.R.* The word is derived from the Czech noun *robota*, which means "labor."

Other notable Czech writers include the nineteenth century writer Božena Němcová and twentieth century writers Ivan Klíma and Josef Škvorecky. Poet Jaroslav Seifert was the first Czech to be awarded the Nobel Prize in literature in 1984. Václav Havel, who was the republic's president from 1989 until 2003, is also a famous writer and playwright.

KAFKA'S GIANT INSECT

Czech writer Franz Kafka is known as one of the most influential authors of the twentieth century. Kafka's novels deal with themes of alienation from society and loneliness. Most of his works were published after his death.
(A Closer Look, page 58)

Arts

Architecture and Art

The Czech Republic is an impressive showcase of European art and architecture through the ages. Gothic architecture, characterized by tall, pointed arches, is exemplified by Prague's St. Vitus's Cathedral. In the sixteenth century, Italians brought their knowledge of Renaissance architecture to Bohemia. In the mid- to late seventeenth century, Baroque architecture made an appearance on the Czech scene. This style is defined by heavy ornamentation and decorative frescoes, which can still be seen today. During the same period, Czech Baroque painting and sculpture also reached a peak. At the end of the nineteenth century, the Czech Art Nouveau style led the architectural scene with buildings decorated in curved floral ironwork. Czech Art Nouveau painter Alphonse Mucha made the style famous abroad. Modern architecture has also made a mark on the country's architectural heritage, particularly in Prague. In 1992, Prague was listed on the United Nations Educational, Scientific and Cultural Organization (UNESCO) World Heritage List.

THE FESTIVAL OF THE FIVE-PETALED ROSE

The medieval town of Český Krumlov comes alive with kings, knights, and princesses once a year to celebrate the past and the dynasty whose emblem is a red flower.
(*A Closer Look, page 54*)

Left: **This Baroque building, one of many found in Prague's Old Town Square, is decorated with scrolls, leaves, statues, and pastel colors.**

Left: **The National Theater, built in the neo-Renaissance style, is a symbol of Czech pride. The first performance at the theater was Smetana's *Libuše*, an opera based on the legendary founding of Prague.**

Drama

Czech theater began as early as the twelfth century and was an important voice for the Czech people. From traditional operas to political satires, theater has reflected the political mood of the country over the years. In 1862, the Provisional Theater opened. It was renamed the National Theater in 1881. After World War II, smaller regional theaters began to open, and, by the late 1950s, theater experienced a wave of revival. Czech stage design, ballet, mime, and puppet theater gained popularity. A new theater form also emerged. Known as Black Light Theater, it makes use of ultraviolet lighting and fluorescent colors to create dramatic effects during performances of mime and puppetry.

Although Czech films were first produced in 1898, Czech filmmaking caught international attention only in the later part of the twentieth century. Czech-born director Miloš Forman won Oscar awards for his films *One Flew over the Cuckoo's Nest* and *Amadeus.* Director Jiří Menzel won an Oscar award for his film *Ostre Šledované Vlaky,* or *Closely Watched Trains.* Every year, the Czech Republic produces about 30 feature films and 1,200 documentaries and cartoons.

Modern film festivals, such as the International Film Festival in Karlovy Vary and the Children's Film Festival in Zlín, are held in the Czech Republic.

CENSORSHIP

Czech theater came under the control and censorship of the Nazis and the Communists during their occupations. The Communists used theater to promote communist theories, and performances and artists that did not adhere to communist principles were banned. The artistic community opposed the Communists, which strongly suppressed Czech artistic culture. This led many Czech artists to flee the country.

MARIONETTES

Dancing, singing, and acting puppets are central to puppet theater. These string-controlled puppets have become a lasting cultural symbol.
(A Closer Look, page 60)

Left: **This bust of Antonín Dvořák marks the famous composer's burial place in Prague's Vyšehrad Cemetery. The son of a butcher and innkeeper, Dvořák wrote nine symphonies and became the first Czech composer who was internationally recognized. Many of Dvořák's works had folk music influences. He died at the age of sixty-two in 1904, shortly after the first Czech musical festival in which he performed his works.**

Music

Music has played a central role in Czech life since the ninth century. During the eleventh century, Czech music was dominated by Gregorian chants and religious hymns. Many of the country's opera houses were built in the eighteenth century. The Nostitz Theater, which was later renamed the Estates Theater, was the venue for the opening nights of some of Mozart's most famous operas, including Don Giovanni, which Mozart conducted in 1787.

The Czech Republic has spawned a number of its own great composers, such as Antonín Dvořák, who wrote *Slavonic Dances* and *Symphony No. 9 (From the New World)*. The latter work was written in 1893, while he was in the United States. Another Czech composer is Bedřich Smetana, who is famous for composing a set of symphonic poems called *My Country*, one of which was inspired by the majestic Vltava river.

The highlight of Czech concert life is the annual Prague Spring International Music Festival. International and local musicians come together from mid-May to early June to perform in this highly anticipated music showcase. The event traditionally opens with Smetana's *My Country* and ends with Beethoven's *Ninth Symphony*. For the rest of the year, there are other music festivals but none as widely acclaimed as Prague Spring.

Jazz music dates back to the 1920s in the Czech Republic. During the Nazi occupation, jazz music was seen as a medium of protest. During the period of Soviet "normalization," many Czech musicians, such as keyboardist Jan Hamr, left the country and found work in the West. Hamr, who escaped to the United States, became prominent in the 1970s under the name Jan Hammer. Since the Velvet Revolution, jazz has experienced a lively revival. Jazz festivals are held annually in a number of towns. Traditional swing and big band jazz remain popular, while newer jazz styles, such as acid jazz and fusion, appeal to younger listeners.

Czech folk music has its origins in the fifteenth century. The composers Bedřich Smetana and Antonín Dvořák were both inspired by Czech folk songs. The polka, a lively form of dance music, originated in eastern Bohemia in the nineteenth century. Folk music is still widely enjoyed in the country today, most often at social gatherings, festivals, and celebrations.

Other styles of music enjoyed in the Czech Republic include pop, rock, reggae, and funk. Prague, in particular, enjoys a variety of international music flavors.

TRADITIONAL COSTUMES

Festivals give modern Czechs the opportunity to wear traditional dress. These elaborate outfits are beautifully detailed and can say a lot about the wearers.
(A Closer Look, page 70)

Below: **Street musicians are common in Prague. They play many styles of music, including classical, folk, and jazz.**

Leisure and Festivals

Sokol

Many Czech families belong to *Sokol* (SOH-kohl), which is a physical education organization that holds regular meetings. Sokol, which means "falcon" in Czech, was founded in 1862 by Czech professor Miroslav Tyrš. Tyrš believed that all forms of sports — and calisthenics and gymnastics, in particular — promote national pride and health in the country's citizens. Sokol has become a important part of Czech culture. Today, the Czech Sokol Organization has 180,000 members in the Czech Republic and supports fifty-seven types of sports. Its popularity has gone beyond the country's boundaries, and Sokol clubs can be found operating in other countries, including Canada and the United States.

Enjoying the Outdoors

The Czech Republic is a winter wonderland. Outdoor ice-skating is a popular activity on the country's frozen ponds and rivers. Downhill skiing and tobogganing in the mountains are also popular activities, as are cross-country skiing and snowboarding.

Below: **Skating and playing ice hockey on the frozen Vltava River are popular winter activities for children.**

During the warmer months, the country's national parks and mountains attract avid hikers, adventurous mountain bikers, and rock climbers. Fishing, canoeing, and swimming in rivers and lakes are popular during the summer. Caving is also enjoyed, especially in the Moravian Karst region.

The country's thermal springs and mineral baths are favorite getaways for both Czechs and foreign tourists. Spa resorts are located in scenic, tranquil areas.

Above: **Retirees play cards and share a meal under the shade of a tree during summer at their *chata* in the Czech countryside.**

Weekend Activities

Urban Czechs wanting to take a break from city life retreat to weekend homes in the countryside. These *chata* (KHAH-tah), or country chalets, are very popular and are very much part of Czech culture. Some weekend homes are traditional rural houses called *chalupa* (KHAH-lu-pah), which are like country cottages. Chalupa are made of wood and are elaborately decorated.

Some families and many retirees spend their weekends or holidays gardening, reading, or playing card games. *Mariáš* (MA-ree-ahsh) is a popular card game, similar to the game of rummy. In late summer or early autumn, Czechs go into the forests to pick *houby* (HO-bay), or mushrooms. This is a favorite traditional Czech pastime. The freshly picked mushrooms are usually cooked and enjoyed on the same day.

Sports

In the Czech Republic, soccer, ice hockey, and tennis are the most popular sports. Czechs also enjoy volleyball and golf. The country has a history of sporting excellence. Many world-famous athletes are Czech.

Soccer is the most popular sport in the country. Czech children can attend soccer training camps during the year. The popular soccer club AC Sparta Praha plays against local soccer teams as well as teams from around Europe. Although the Czech soccer team performed well in the 1996 European championship, it has been over four decades since the team made a strong showing in World Cup competition.

Ice hockey is also a popular national sport. The former Czechoslovak national ice hockey teams have been ranked among the top six national teams in the world. The Czech Republic's national ice hockey team won ten World Hockey Championships and a 1998 Olympic gold medal. Jaromír Jágr and Dominik Hašek are two famous Czech ice hockey players.

Czech athletes have made their marks in other areas of international competition as well. Runner Emil Zátopek set eighteen world records during his track-and-field career and won four Olympic gold medals. Gymnast Věra Čáslavská was

Left: **Czech javelin thrower Jan Železný is the only three-time gold medal javelin winner in Olympic history.**

Left: Ivan Lendl is said to be among the best male tennis players in tennis history. He was ranked first for a record-breaking 270 consecutive weeks.

a multiple Olympic medal winner during the 1964 and 1968 Olympics. Javelin-thrower Dana Zátopková, decathlete Tomáš Dvořák, and triple-jumper Šárka Kašpárková are well-known Czech athletes who recently have brought home Olympic medals. In 2000, Štěpánka Hilgertová won a gold medal in the Olympics for women's slalom canoeing, and Aleš Valenta emerged champion in the 2002 Olympics for freestyle skiing, setting a world record with his performance. In the arena of cycling, cross-country bikers Miloš Fiséra and Radomir Šimůnek won numerous world champion titles. Brothers Jan and Jindřich Pospíšil, have dominated bicycle polo with their twenty world championship titles. Czech cyclist Vitězslav Dostál rode his Czech-made bike around the world on a three-year bike tour.

Tennis

Because of famous Czech tennis players such as Martina Navrátilová and Ivan Lendl, tennis has gained popularity in the Czech Republic. Indoor and outdoor tennis courts and organized tennis clubs can be found all over the country. Young tennis enthusiasts can attend tennis camps and learn from professional coaches. Some of the Czech Republic's tennis players are among the top one hundred international tennis players.

TENNIS LEGEND MARTINA NAVRÁTILOVÁ

Martina Navrátilová has set several records in her tennis career. She is considered to have been one of the best female tennis players in the world.

(*A Closer Look*, page 68)

Left: **Boys used to make their own pomlázkas, but now ready-made ones can be bought at a store. The Easter fun, however, still continues when they look for women to playfully swat. According to tradition, the braided willow branches will bring health and youth to anyone swatted with them.**

Festivals

Festivals are celebrated throughout the year in the Czech Republic. Some of these festivals are religious, but when they were celebrated during the communist years, their traditional meanings were suppressed. Since 1989, the religious origins of these holidays have been rediscovered.

Every day of the year is a celebration for somebody in the Czech Republic. This is because each day is a different person's "name day." It is customary to celebrate a friend's name day by giving them flowers or chocolates and wishing them "Happy Name Day!" March 19, for example, is the name day for Josef, a common male name in the country.

Easter is a colorful and joyous time in the Czech Republic. The week before Easter is full of activity. Boys go through the streets making loud noises with wooden rattles. On Easter Sunday, girls make elaborately decorated eggs called *kraslice* (KRAH-slih-zee), and boys braid willow branches together to form a *pomlázka* (PO-mlah-skah). On Easter Monday, they use their pomlázkas to gently swat women, who give the boys kraslice. A girl will give her most beautiful egg to her to her favorite boy, and she will tie a ribbon to his pomlázka.

CZECH BELIEFS AND SUPERSTITIONS

Czechs have beliefs connected to special occasions. Many Czechs also perform special actions that are meant to ensure luck or prevent an untimely death.

(*A Closer Look,* page 52)

May Day is the day of love. On the evening of May 1, lovers gather in Prague's Petřín Park to lay flowers at the statue of the great romantic poet Karel Hynek Mácha, the unofficial patron of lovers. His famous poem *May* tells of the tragic love of two young people.

Christmas

At the beginning of the Christmas season, families pick branches from morello cherry trees and keep them in warm places so that they blossom before Christmas. Christmas festivities begin with *Mikuláš*, or Saint Nicholas Day, which falls on December 6. On the eve of Mikuláš, children await the arrival of Saint Nicholas. He is said to reward good children with small gifts and candy. Bad children receive potatoes, coal, or a rock.

On Christmas Eve, families meet for a traditional Christmas dinner of carp and potato salad. The carp is usually bought live a few days before Christmas and can be kept in the family's bathtub until it is time for it to be cooked. After dinner, family members exchange presents. December 25 and 26 are also holidays, and Czech families spend these days together.

"GOOD KING WENCESLAS"

In the Czech Republic, "Good King Wenceslas" is more than a Christmas carol that people sing during yuletide festivities. Wenceslas was an actual duke who ruled the Czech lands centuries ago.
(A Closer Look, page 56)

Left: **Carp are sold in huge tanks at the market. Some families buy two carp, one for the traditional Christmas dinner and one to be released into a river after Christmas.**

39

Food

Czech cuisine has been shaped by Celtic and Slavonic influences, as well as by favorite foods in neighboring countries. For example, German sauerkraut and dumplings are widely enjoyed, as is Hungarian goulash.

A typical Czech meal is heavy with meats and rich sauces. Main meals usually include a type of meat, such as pork, beef, rabbit, or wild fowl. Pond-bred trout and carp are also used. The main meal is usually served with potatoes, rice, or dumplings. Sauerkraut is usually a sidedish but is also used in soup. Fried mushrooms are also a popular accompaniment. A common Czech main dish is *Veprŏ-knedlo-zelo* (vepro-KNED-loh-ZEE-loh), or roast pork served with dumplings and sauerkraut. Another favorite is *Svíčková* (SVEETCH-ko-vah), or sliced beef sirloin.

Dumplings are common in Czech cuisine. They can be made with potatoes or bread. Dumplings can be eaten as a side dish, as a main meal, and even as a dessert when they are filled with fruit, such as blueberries.

Czech meals begin with soup, followed by the main course, a salad, and, finally, dessert. Popular soups are potato soup and liver dumpling soup. Desserts include fruit dumplings, apple strudel, crepes, tarts, and pancakes.

Left: **A waiter prepares a dessert crepe. Eating out is not common and is reserved for special occasions. This custom is slowly changing, however, with the younger generation.**

Above: Hospoda (HO-spo-dah), or beer halls, are social places for Czechs who prefer to drink among friends.

Typically, the main meal of the day is eaten at lunch time. Czechs usually have only a cup of coffee and rolls for breakfast. In the evening, dinners are light and consist of breads, cured meats, and assorted Czech cheeses.

Drinks are usually served after the meal and not before or during. Fruit juices and sodas are popular with children. For adults, the most common drink is *pivo* (PEE-vo), or beer. Herbal liquors, plum brandy, and Moravian wines are favored by Czech adults, as well.

Table etiquette is important to Czechs. Making slurping noises while eating is considered bad manners.

Beer Culture

Czech cuisine is often followed by a Czech beer, which is often less expensive than sodas. The country is famous for Pilsner beer, which is named after the town of Plzeň. Another popular brew is Budweiser Budvar. A typical Czech drinks about 42 gallons (160 liters) of beer each year; Czechs consume the most beer per capita in the world. There are over seventy breweries in the country that make different types of beer, including diet beers, with various colors and concentrations of alcohol. Dark beer is sweet, and light beer is bitter. Most Czechs prefer light beer.

A CLOSER LOOK AT THE CZECH REPUBLIC

A visitor to the Czech Republic today will observe a country rich in culture, art, and national pride. The country's heritage has been enriched by the strength of the many individuals who have helped to shape the republic's history. Famous leaders — such as Saint Wenceslas, the "good" King, and Václav Havel, a major leader of the Velvet Revolution— acted on their convictions and took their country in new directions. Today, statues and monuments honor them. Talented artists and sports personalities have also helped to keep their country in the international spotlight over the decades.

Opposite: **St. Vitus's Cathedral in Prague doubles as a venue for one of the many concerts of the Prague Spring International Music Festival.**

One aspect of Czech heritage that has survived the ages is its advanced level of craftsmanship. Small manufacturers still produce and sell handmade crystal chandeliers and glassware. Wooden marionettes are also handmade by artisans.

Czechs know how to have fun. The many festivals celebrated by locals throughout the year often involve the wearing of fancy traditional clothes and are colorful events. They reflect the strong sense of tradition still seen in most Czechs today, while showcasing the nation's love for music, drama, and dance.

Above: **Kings, queens, and even moustached bandits can become part of a puppeteer's performance. Puppets are part of the country's rich cultural heritage.**

43

Acid Rain

In the latter half of the twentieth century, heavy industrialization and the use of coal-powered factories caused acid rain to form. An environmental hazard, acid rain fell over large portions of Czech forests, mostly in northern Bohemia, and caused widespread damage.

What is Acid Rain?

Acid rain is formed when sulfur dioxide and nitrous oxide combine with moisture in the atmosphere and on the surface of vegetation to form sulfuric acid and nitric acid. These oxides come from industrial emissions produced by coal-burning power stations, factories, and industrial plants fueled by natural gas or oil, as well as exhaust fumes from gasoline-powered vehicles.

When rain containing sulfuric and nitric acids falls onto soil, the soil becomes acidic and damages tree roots. The damaged roots are unable to absorb enough nutrients for proper growth, and the trees in the soil eventually die. Acid rain also turns leaves yellow, interfering with photosynthesis. This problem also causes trees to die. In addition, when acid rain falls onto lakes, rivers, and streams, the plants and animals that depend on them are

Left: **Acid rain has heavily damaged about two-thirds of the forests in the Black Triangle region, leaving nothing but dead trees behind. Acid rain affects crops as well. When crops are damaged, agricultural yields fall.**

Left: **Chemicals that cause air pollution, and, ultimately, acid rain are released into the air by the factories located in the Black Triangle. The air in this area can get so thick with smoke that visibility is reduced.**

affected. The problem is more serious in the spring when contaminated snow melts into the country's waterways. When acid rain falls onto buildings and bridges, it causes deterioration. Architectural details can be lost because of the corrosive effect of acid rain. Acid contained in the form of smog can also harm people with respiratory problems such as asthma or bronchitis.

The Black Triangle

The Black Triangle is an infamous area that has been heavily affected by acid rain. Located at the intersection of Poland, Germany, and the Czech Republic, it is one of Europe's most industrialized, and also most polluted, areas. Pollution levels there were found to be between five and ten times higher than acceptable levels. As a result, many woodlands and forests now are barren and dotted with dead or dying trees. Some rivers have not been able to support aquatic life for decades.

Since 1991, the governments of the Czech Republic, Germany, and Poland have taken steps toward reducing industrial emissions in the Black Triangle. Today, there are signs that the ecosystem is recovering.

The Angry Vltava

The Vltava , the Czech Republic's longest river, was once used to transport timber that was used for building towns and castles out of the forests from which it was harvested. Today, the river is used for recreation and sight-seeing. Its serene waters, however, mask a more turbulent nature. The river has periodically overflowed its banks causing widespread flooding and destruction. A hint of its destructive potential is found in the river's name, which comes from the German word that means "wild, strong water."

The Great Flood

In the summer of 2002, the country was witness to the mighty river at one of its angriest moments, and the Czech Republic experienced what some reports called its worst flooding in 200 years. Over 200,000 people were evacuated from their homes, and a state of emergency was declared in Prague and central Bohemia. Floodwaters rose 6 inches (15 cm) per hour, and the Vltava was 22 feet (7 m) above its usual level. At forty times the volume of water the river normally carries, the raging flood swept away trees and other structures and slammed them against bridges and buildings.

THE VLTAVA'S LONG JOURNEY

The Vltava has its source in the Šumava Mountains. From an elevation of 3,845 feet (1,172 m) above sea level, it flows northward, passing through many historical towns and the city of Prague before it joins with the Labe River. The length of the Vltava River (from its source to the point at which it joins the Labe River) is 270 miles (435 km).

Left: A swan swims in what used to be a traffic-congested Prague street. After the flood, some streets could only be accessed by boat.

In Prague, buildings near the river were submerged under water. Many of Prague's museums and historical buildings had muddy water up to their second floors. Precious books and artifacts kept in storage basements were damaged by water, sewage, and mud.

Traffic, electricity, and gas were disrupted for days. Several city subway stations were completely flooded. The statue of composer Bedřich Smetana, who is known for his symphonic poem about the Vltava, was nearly submerged. Elsewhere, entire towns and villages along the Vltava were almost completely submerged. Rooftops were the only visible evidence of the buildings beneath the water.

Eighteen people in the country died as a result of the angry Vltava. Many Czechs faced the risk of collapsing buildings and disease carried by the flood. It took three weeks before the swollen river eased and receded, leaving Prague residents scurrying to drain buildings filled with cultural treasures and to clean up their mud-filled city.

Several dams had been constructed along the Vltava to act as flood control and to provide hydroelectric power to the country. During the 2002 flood, however, these systems turned out to be inadequate to protect the country from serious damage.

Bohemian Crystal and Glass

The Czech Republic is famous for its glass and crystal. The country began decorative glass production in the thirteenth century, while crystal was invented only later in the eighteenth century. Crystal is formed when lead is mixed with high quality glass to form a clear surface that is hard enough to be engraved or cut. While the glass is hot, it is blown into molds that form it into various shapes, after which it is cut and engraved. Elaborate crystal pieces have many facets and are shiny. Bohemian crystal is unique for two reasons. First, it has a high lead content, and second, the engraved designs are usually intricately detailed.

The History of Czech Glass

Early glass production in the region began with small glass beads that were used for jewelry. By the early fifteenth century, glass foundries began operating in Bohemia, producing what was

Below: **A craftsman carves out intricate patterns on a vase. The Czech Republic has a strong tradition of crystal-making.**

known as "forest glass." This glass was so named because it had a light green color as a result of imperfections during its manufacture. Bohemian crystal was invented when Czech crystal manufacturers discovered that adding chalk to the crystal made it clearer and easier to engrave. The Venetians, who at the time were leading the crystal market, felt threatened by the popularity of this new competitor and banned the import of Bohemian crystal.

In the early nineteenth century, Bohemian glassmakers began deliberately putting color into their products in an attempt to outdo other European glass producers. At this time, many Czech glassmakers began to work abroad and were part of a growing international glass and crystal industry.

The glass and crystal industry in the Czech Republic survived both the Nazi occupation and communism, during which most glass factories were converted to produce practical glass items, such as television screens, optical lenses, and drinking glasses. Many craftsmen practiced their art and maintained their skills in secret, with some producing pieces of art that came to be known as glass sculpture. Since the Velvet Revolution in 1989, the Bohemian crystal industry has enjoyed a healthy revival. Today, about forty-eight factories supply the country's export and tourist markets. Jablonec nad Nisou and Česká Lípa in northern Bohemia are two main centers for the Bohemian crystal industry.

SWAROVSKI CRYSTAL

One of the most famous European producers of crystal today is the Swarovski company, which was founded by Czech Daniel Swarovski. Swarovski learned to manually cut crystals from his father. Inspired by an exhibition on electrical machinery, he invented a crystal-cutting machine that was fast and could produce accurate work. In 1895, Swarovski set up his company in Austria and continued to develop the perfect crystal. In 1913, Swarovski met with success. His flawless crystal was bought by French fashion houses and jewelers. Today, Swarovski crystal is sold all over the world.

The Children of Terezín

Located 37 miles (60 km) north of Prague, the town of Terezín became a ghetto and concentration camp for Jews during World War II. The Germans called the town "Theresienstadt." Elderly people, families, and a great number of artists and intellectuals were forced by the Germans to move to Terezín. Most of them were Czech Jews sent there for "safekeeping." Many of the people who were held there were later transported to Auschwitz, where most of them were killed.

Conditions in Terezín were horrific, and many died there of diseases or malnutrition. Before the war, fewer than 5,000 people were living in Terezín. The first year the Nazis turned the town into a ghetto, about 60,000 people were forced to live in it. Of the 140,000 people that passed through the camp, about 15,000 were children under the age of fifteen. By the end of the war, only about 100 of these children survived.

AUSCHWITZ

Located in Poland, Auschwitz became a Nazi concentration camp during World War II. Many Jewish prisoners, including children, were sent to Auschwitz and murdered in the camp's gas chambers.

Below: **The courtyard in the Terezín ghetto was used by the Nazis for the public execution of many Czech Jews.**

Left: **A painting of a sailboat by a Terezín child. The works by the Terezín children provide hints of how they coped with the harsh life in the concentration camp .**

Life in Terezín

Because teaching was not permitted, the children of Terezín attended informal lectures by some of the adults, who also put on occasional theater performances, such as the children's opera *Brundibar.* The opera was about two children and an evil organ player. *Brundibar* was a favorite, and the children in Terezín knew the organ player represented Adolf Hitler. The children also spent time drawing and writing poetry on paper smuggled to them by the adult artists. Their works showed their fears and the bad conditions in which they were living. For some, their works illustrated their hopes for a better future. A great number of these children died just a year before the war ended.

During World War II, the Red Cross was permitted to visit Terezín. The Nazis placed specially dressed prisoners at strategic points and hid those worst affected by famine and disease. Terezín was used as a model ghetto for a Nazi propaganda film that showed healthy Jews enjoying a rich cultural life.

After the war, more than 4,000 drawings and poems by the children of Terezín were found in two suitcases. The children's art teacher hid these works before she was sent off to Auschwitz. The drawings and poems are now owned by the Jewish Museum in Prague and many are displayed at Terezín, which is now a museum.

FRIEDL DICKER-BRANDEIS (1898–1944)

Friedl Dicker-Brandeis was the children's art teacher in Terezín. She believed that art would help the children express their emotions and enable them to cope with the bad conditions of the ghetto. She was later sent to Auschwitz and died there.

Czech Beliefs and Superstitions

The Czech people, particularly those living in rural areas, are superstitious. This is especially true during special celebrations, such as Easter and Christmas, as well as on weddings and birthdays.

During the week leading up to Easter, Czech women busy themselves cleaning floors, furniture, and curtains. Beating their quilts and mattresses outdoors is said to rid the house of any sickness. On the Wednesday before Easter, also known as Ugly Wednesday, many people eat honey with bread because they believe this will protect them from snake bites in the year ahead. It is also a day on which everyone smiles at each other, because it is believed that anyone found frowning will be frowning every Wednesday for the whole year! On Good Friday, people wake up early and hurry down to a brook, stream, or river. There, they wash themselves with cold water and cross the water with bare legs. They believe that doing this ensures good health for the next year.

THE WATER GOBLIN

One Czech legend warns children about the evil Water Goblin, who lives at the bottom of ponds and lakes. Parents tell their children not to get too close to the water's edge because the Water Goblin will take their souls away forever. This superstition was first recorded by Karel J. Erben and was immortalized by Antonín Dvořák, who wrote a symphonic poem about the Water Goblin legend.

Left: Czechs welcome the start of spring by throwing a dummy of the goddess Morana into the river. Morana is believed to be the goddess of winter.

When a couple marries, the bride's friends will plant a tree in her yard and decorate it with ribbons and eggshells. The tree is thought to indicate how long the bride will live. If the tree dies early, it is believed that the bride will die young.

On Christmas Eve

According to superstition, Christmas Eve is the best time to predict the future. Before dinner begins, the head of the family cuts a loaf of bread and passes out the slices. If there are slices left over, then family members expect new arrivals to the family. If there is a slice missing, then the family anticipates that a member of the family may die. After the meal, an apple is cut. The shape of the apple core is believed to tell what kind of future a person will have. A cross means illness or death, while a star signifies good luck. After dinner, everyone gets up from the table at the same time, since it is believed that whoever stands up first will die within one year. For young women, Christmas is a time to predict when they will marry. The women throw their shoes over their heads. If the shoe points to the door, it is thought that a wedding is likely to happen soon. If a girl is curious about her future husband, she picks a log from a log pile; a superstition says that the shape of the wood tells her how slim or fat her future spouse will be.

GIVING FLOWERS

For birthdays and name days, it is considered bad luck to receive an even number of flowers. Even-numbered bouquets are only used at funerals.

The Festival of the Five-Petaled Rose

The Festival of the Five-Petaled Rose is a Renaissance celebration held in the beautiful town of Český Krumlov in June of each year. The celebration lasts for three days, and the streets of Český Krumlov fill with people dressed as knights, courtiers, jugglers, artisans, musicians, and merchants. Dramatized fencing contests, chess matches, classical and historical music performances, craft demonstrations, and plays entertain the townspeople and visiting tourists. People wearing Renaissance finery stroll through the gardens of Český Krumlov's castle to meet and greet the many guests. Medieval feasts are also held in the streets, where roast pig, chicken, wine, and beer are served. In the evening, the festival features fireworks displays. Folk music and dancing complete the festivities.

The Festival of The Five-Petaled Rose was introduced in 1985 in honor of the Rožmberk dynasty, one of the most noble and influential of Czech families. The castle was the family's residence, and Český Krumlov was the family's estate. Under

Left: **Czech revelers in elaborate medieval and Renaissance costumes celebrate in the streets of Cesky Krumlov.**

their rule, the town flourished, reaching its peak during the Renaissance period. The festival is named after the emblem of the Rožmberk dynasty — a red five-petaled rose.

Above: Český Krumlov is almost entirely encircled by a tight meander in the Vltava River. The town is a living museum of the country's architecture throughout the ages.

The Town of Český Krumlov

Český Krumlov derived its name from the old German term which means "crooked shaped meadow," a reference to its location at the meander of the Vltava River. Český Krumlov is a historic town and an architectural treasure, which makes the backdrop of the Festival of the Five-Petaled Rose as authentic as it is beautiful. At the center of the town stands the thirteenth-century Rožmberk castle, which exhibits a mix of Gothic, Renaissance, and Baroque architectural styles. In 1992, Český Krumlov was recognized as a fine example of a small, central European medieval town and was named a UNESCO World Heritage site. The town has remained intact for more than five centuries and has about 300 buildings of historical value. In addition to the Festival of the Five-Petaled Rose, Český Krumlov hosts a number of other festivals.

"Good King Wenceslas"

The famous Christmas carol "Good King Wenceslas" tells about the kind and generous spirit of a real person in history — a Czech ruler of the Přemysl dynasty. In the Christmas carol, Wenceslas notices a poor man gathering firewood on the day after Christmas, which is known as the Feast of Stephen. Determined to help the man, the king and his servant set out in the cold to help the man. When the servant is too cold to continue, King Wenceslas takes the lead and urges his servant to follow him.

Wenceslas, Duke of Bohemia

In A.D. 907, Wenceslas was born to the duke and duchess of Bohemia and was raised by his devout Christian grandmother, Ludmila. Wenceslas was only thirteen years old when his father died, and he succeeded his father as duke. Because of his young age, his mother, Drahomíra, assumed control. Drahomíra opposed Christianity and persecuted many Christians. She was deeply concerned about Ludmila's influence over Wenceslas

Left: **The relationship between young Wenceslas and his grandmother, Ludmila, (*right*) shaped his values and morals. Their closeness is depicted in this statue found along Charles Bridge in Prague.**

Left: **The Chapel of Saint Wenceslas is home to the Czech crown jewels, which are kept in a vault in a corner of the beautiful chapel. Seven different locks secure the vault. Each key is kept by a different person, and all seven of them must be present for the vault to be opened.**

and eventually arranged for Ludmila to be murdered. When Wenceslas reached the age of eighteen, he removed his mother from power and took control over Bohemia.

As a ruler, Wenceslas was passionate about protecting the rights of Christians and the poor. Renowned for his generosity and kindness, he was particularly fond of children, especially orphans, and went out of his way to help protect them from slavery. Wenceslas also believed that in order to promote the influence of Christianity, the country had to form alliances with other Christian countries, including Germany. This policy angered the Bohemian nobility, and they prompted his younger brother, Boleslav, to kill him. On September 28 of A.D 929, Boleslav assassinated Wenceslas as he was making his way to church. Soon after his death, Wenceslas was proclaimed a saint. His remains were transferred to St. Vitus's Cathedral in Prague.

Saint Wenceslas Day

Saint Wenceslas is the patron saint of the Czech Republic and is remembered for his generosity and fairness as a leader. Saint Wenceslas Day falls on September 28, which was the date of his murder. It is a national holiday in the Czech Republic.

HONORING A GOOD KING

Saint Wenceslas is literally a central figure in Prague. To commemorate his deeds, a statue of the good duke atop a horse was erected. The statue faces a square also named in his honor. Wenceslas Square has been the center of many of the country's most historic events.

Kafka's Giant Insect

Imagine going to sleep and waking up in your family home as a giant insect! Czech writer Franz Kafka wrote about a transformation like this in his novella *The Metamorphosis* (1915).

The story is about a young man by the name of Gregor Samsa, who lives with his family and works as a traveling salesman. He is the sole provider for his mother, father, and younger sister. One morning he wakes up to find that he has become a giant insect. Not only does he look strange, he also begins to take on the behavior of a bug. Gregor faces rejection by his family when his appearance and behavior change. He is confined to his bedroom and only his younger sister cares enough to bring him food. One day, Gregor's angry father throws an apple at his changed son and injures him. Gregor eventually dies as a result of an infected wound and is thrown into the garbage.

The grotesque imagery used in this story is typical of Kafka's writing. Gregor's transformation expresses Kafka's view that human existence is insecure. Anything, he believed, can happen at any time, entirely without reason.

Left: **British actor and playwright Steven Berkoff portrays the character of Gregor Samsa, who turned into an insect in Kafka's story.**

Franz Kafka (1883-1924)

Franz Kafka was the son of a Jewish shopkeeper. In 1906, he obtained a law degree and took a job in an insurance company. Two years later, he joined the partly government-owned Workers' Accident Insurance Institute. He considered his jobs merely a way to earn a living. Writing was his first love. In 1917, Kafka became ill with tuberculosis and took frequent periods of leave to rest. The writer spent much time after 1917 in sanatoriums and health resorts because of his ailing condition. He finally retired in 1922 and died two years later.

Below: Young Franz Kafka was shy and thoughtful. He spent his time writing while helping his father with the family business.

Kafka was reluctant to publish his work, only publishing a few of his earlier works, such as *The Judgment* (1912), *Meditation* (1913), *The Metamorphosis* (1915), *The Penal Colony* (1919), and *A Country Doctor* (1919), during his lifetime. He left instructions that any unpublished manuscripts should be destroyed upon his death. His longtime friend Max Brod, however, arranged for them to be published. Kafka became one of the most influential writers of the twentieth century in the years after his death. Some of his most famous novels, originally written in German and later translated, are *The Trial* (1925), *The Castle* (1926), and *Amerika* (1927).

Marionettes

A marionette is a puppet that has a movable head and jointed limbs, all of which a puppeteer controls from above, using strings attached to each part. String marionettes originated in Italy and were introduced to the Czech region in 1563. Since then, they have become an important part of Czech culture.

Early Puppeteers

In the seventeenth and eighteenth centuries, marionette theater enjoyed great popularity among rural Czechs as an affordable form of family entertainment. Families of puppeteers would travel from village to village, and their collections of marionettes would be pushed along in carts or wheelbarrows. Early puppeteers tended to perform for peasant communities throughout the countryside because they were not allowed to perform in the cities. Aside from telling stories of kings, queens, knights, and princesses, puppeteers sometimes also included the latest news

Below: **Czech marionettes often represent characters from the country's history and folktales. Some characters look comical, while others look fearsome.**

Left: **Famous Czech marionette characters include (*from left to right*) Mánička, Hurvínek, Spejbl, Švejk, and Pinocchio. Two other comical characters that emerged and became important symbols of Czech puppetry are Škrhola, the village idiot, and Kašparek, or Pimprle, the jester. These two characters are loved by children because of their funny antics.**

or social commentary in their performances. Members of the Bohemian nobility were often featured, and authority figures were mocked. Puppeteers also included legends and different superstitions from the Czech oral tradition in their shows. They helped to preserve these stories through countless retellings to different audiences in the country. Later, as children became the main audience at marionette performances, many puppeteers added folk and fairy tales to their shows.

Modern Marionettes

Today, the Czech Republic boasts a thriving marionette industry. Marionette makers produce puppets ranging from traditional characters to contemporary figures, including representations of famous modern people. Many of Prague's museums house collections of prized historical Czech marionettes. Modern reproductions of famous Czech marionettes, however, are sold nearly everywhere in Prague. Puppeteers in the country's many marionette theaters continue to captivate both adults and children. Every June, Prague hosts the World Festival of Puppet Art. The festival showcases all sorts of marionettes and new developments in the art of puppetry.

Not Just Any Castle

More than a former king's place of residence and work, Prague Castle still features prominently in modern Czech life as the country's political center and the seat of the Czech government.

Built by Prince Bořivoj of the Přemysl dynasty in the ninth century, Prague Castle is the world's largest ancient castle, covering an area of 18 acres (7 hectares). Located within the castle's walls is a complex of different buildings that includes three palaces, a cathedral, a number of churches and monasteries, and even a convent. The castle has undergone numerous reconstructions and additions, which have left visible reminders of every historical period on its premises. Today, the castle is a mixture of Gothic, Romanesque, Renaissance, and Baroque architecture, as well as nineteenth- and twentieth-century styles. In 1918, the castle became the home of the country's first president, Tomáš G. Masaryk. Modifications made to parts of the castle later created space for government offices.

Below: **The Lobkowicz Palace is one of the three palaces that are found on the sprawling grounds of Prague Castle. The other two palaces are the Royal Palace and the Royal Summer Palace.**

Left: Located at the base of the castle's walls is the Golden Lane. This street was named after the seventeenth-century goldsmiths' houses that dominated the area. These houses were originally the dwellings of the castle servants. In the early twentieth century, the area was home to writer Franz Kafka and poet Jaroslav Seifert. Kafka lived there from 1916 to 1917.

St. Vitus's Cathedral

At the heart of the royal compound is the late Gothic-style St. Vitus's Cathedral, which was commissioned by Emperor Charles IV in 1344. The cathedral was begun by Matthias of Arras and completed by Petr Parléř. Later additions to it were made in the Renaissance and Baroque styles. The cathedral houses the remains of many of the region's most influential leaders, including St. Wenceslas and Charles IV. Also known as the St. Wenceslas crown, the country's coronation crown, which is used only for formal ceremonies, is kept there. The impressive Chapel of St. Wenceslas, which is famous for being decorated with gems, is also found within the cathedral.

The Royal Palace

The Royal Palace is one of the oldest parts of Prague Castle. Built in 1135, it originally was the residence of the Bohemian princes and later became the king's palace. Its Vladislav Hall was once used for coronations and royal festivities. Today, this hall is used for important gatherings and the swearing in of the country's president. Near this hall is a room with the notorious window at which the second Defenestration took place.

THE CASTLE TOWERS

Prague Castle's towers were built for defensive purposes, but they have also served as prisons, workshops, a laboratory, and a gunpowder store. Today, the towers and many of the Castle's buildings are museums, housing art collections and even the second-largest toy museum in the world.

The Princess-Nun

Princess Agnes

The daughter of Přemysl king Ottokar I, Agnes was betrothed to Boleslaus, the son of Henry, Duke of Silesia, when she was a young girl and was sent to Silesia to be educated. Three years after her arrival, however, her young husband-to-be died. Agnes then returned to Bohemia and continued her education in a convent. A few years later, she was betrothed to Henry, son of Emperor Frederick II. Henry, however, chose to marry the daughter of an Austrian duke. Agnes was happy when she heard the news because she wanted to join a convent. Years later, Emperor Frederick II's wife, Jolante, died and he proposed marriage to Agnes, who was twenty-eight by that time. Not

Left: **Betrothed twice to prominent nobles and finally to an emperor, Saint Agnes of Bohemia chose a life of poverty and charity.**

Left: Located along the Vltava River in Prague's Old Town, the convent Saint Agnes founded has been renamed the Convent of Saint Agnes of Bohemia. The convent is Prague's oldest Gothic structure and is visited by many tourists each year. The convent currently houses a collection of medieval and early Renaissance Czech art that belongs to Prague's National Gallery.

wanting to wed the emperor, Agnes asked Pope Gregory IX to help her. The emperor was angry when Agnes refused to marry him, but he said he must accept her calling by the king of heaven.

Life as a Nun

Agnes was finally free to follow her chosen religious path. The princess gave up her worldly belongings and devoted her life to helping the poor and sick. She established the first Convent of Poor Clares in Prague. The order of Poor Clares was founded by Clare of Assisi, who insisted on a life of rugged poverty for those wishing to follow the order. Agnes never met Clare, who later became a saint, but they exchanged letters and became friends.

Over her lifetime, Agnes was known for her humility and dedication to the plight of the poor, as well as her courage and faith. Many people respected and admired her; they knew that she was a royal princess who had sacrificed her wealth for the sake of her religion. Her life inspired hundreds of young noble women to join the order of the Poor Clares, and many more to establish and support convents around the country.

Agnes died in March 1282 at the age of seventy-seven. She was canonized in November 1989 by Pope John Paul II. In the Czech Republic, she is known as *Anežka Česká*.

The Surefooted Chamois

The chamois is a type of mountain antelope. A small population of these beasts inhabits the mountains of the Czech Republic. Nimble and hardy, the chamois is famous for its impressive leaping ability. It is so well adapted to its living environment that its hooves are able to cling to rocky surfaces, and its soft elastic soles prevent it from slipping.

Chamois are usually about the size of large goats, with males generally being heavier than females. Both sexes, however, have sharp horns that curve backward near the tips that they use mainly to defend themselves against predators. Chamois have two distinctive coats during the year: a mostly brown summer coat and a thick, blackish winter coat with white markings on its underside. Chamois also characteristically have black markings on their faces and small, black tails.

Below: **The chamois is herbivorous, meaning that it eats only plants. It is known to favor grass and flowers in summer and lichens, grass, and small plants in the winter. Lichens are unusual plants that consist of fungi and algae growing together and look like crusty patches on tree trunks or rocks.**

Living Habits

During spring and autumn, chamois roam the alpine forests high up in the mountains. In summer, the animals retreat even farther up the mountainside to escape the heat. During winter, however, chamois travel down to the lower slopes where plants, such as grass shoots, are more plentiful. Female and young chamois tend to live in small herds. Male chamoix tend to be solitary, joining herds only during the chamois rut.

Declining Numbers

Chamois once roamed the Czech mountainside in abundance. Apart from being eaten by their natural predators, such as wolves, lynxes, and eagles, chamois hunting by humans has contributed much to the species's decline. The animal's meat is highly prized, and its pelt, or skin, is the source of valuable chamois leather, which is used to make coats and jackets. The tufts of hair along the animal's back are used to make hunters' caps. The shammy cloth, which is widely used for polishing glass and cars, was inspired by chamois leather.

Above: **Female chamois tend to travel with their young in small herds. In winter, when food is scarce, they look for food at lower altitudes, where they risk being hunted by both other animals and humans.**

THE CHAMOIS RUT

The chamois rut occurs from mid-October to December. During the rut, the males lock horns and fight for mates. The winners gets to mate with a female chamois. If mating is successful, a female chamois will give birth in the spring. She usually produces only one or two offspring from each pregnancy.

Tennis Legend
Martina Navrátilová

Tennis player Martina Navrátilová has been described as one of the world's greatest athletes in the twentieth century. By the time she retired from singles tennis in 1994, she had amassed a staggering number of records, winning 167 singles titles, 9 Wimbledon championships, and more singles matches than anyone in tennis history

Navrátilová was ranked number one in the world seven times and was among the world's top five players for eighteen years. She won eighteen Grand Slam singles titles, including her record nine Wimbledon crowns, four U.S. Opens, two French Opens, and three Australian Opens. At one point, she held the number one ranking for women's singles for 331 weeks.

The Early Years

Navrátilová was born in Prague on October 18, 1956. She spent her early childhood in the Krkonoše Mountains. Her stepfather Mírek Navrátil coached her in tennis. By the age of eight, Navrátilová was winning tennis tournaments and began taking lessons with George Parma, who was a leading Czech tennis

Left: **Návratilová competes at Wimbledon in 1980.**

player at that time. In 1973, Navrátilová became a professional tennis player. She made her first visit to the United States that same year. Navrátilová was outspoken about her political views, which spurred the communist Czechoslovak sports authorities to restrict her travel to the United States. In 1975, at age nineteen, Navrátilová made the difficult decision of leaving home and seeking political asylum in the United States so that she could pursue her tennis career. In 1981, Navrátilová became a U.S. citizen and began a winning streak that lasted for fourteen years.

Winning Style

Navrátilová is credited with reinventing women's tennis. Her aggressive serve-and-volley approach and her focus soon became the hallmarks of her tennis style. In 1994, after playing professional tennis for twenty-two years, she retired from playing singles. She is still, however, active on the tennis circuit and continues to accumulate victories playing doubles. Navrátilová also actively supports a number of nonprofit organizations and charitable causes.

NAVRÁTILOVÁ VS. EVERT

Navrátilová's friendly rivalry with fellow tennis player Chris Evert was a highlight of women's tennis in the 1970s and 1980s. From 1973 to 1988, they played eighty matches against each other, and Navrátilová led the rivalry 43-37. The competitive relationship between Navrátilová and Evert remains the longest and most outstanding in women's tennis history.

Traditional Costumes

During the country's many folk festivals and celebrations, Czechs exchange their everyday modern clothes for *kroje* (KRO-yih), or traditional costumes. Czech traditional costumes vary from region to region. Each tells a story. The design of the costume, the types and colors of the fabrics used, and the patterns that decorate them indicate a costume's place of origin, as well as the age and marital status of the wearer. Married women, for example, commonly wear embroidered caps or headscarves, while unmarried girls may wear flowers in their hair. For men, bachelors wear long feathers in their hats that are clipped short when they get married.

Women's Finery

A woman's kroje consists of a linen or cotton blouse with puffy sleeves, a vest with trimmings, a woven skirt with an apron over the top, knitted socks, and leather shoes or boots. In Bohemia, traditional costumes are often made of more expensive materials, such as silk and wool, which reflect the wealth and nobility common in the region.

Left: **Each of these three women are wearing a different traditional costume. In Bohemia, most people stopped wearing kroje by the late 1800s, but in Moravia, kroje remained everyday apparel until the 1930s.**

The color of the embroidery on the wearer's blouse or apron also indicates the region from which the wearer comes. Costumes from Moravia tend to be embroidered with black threads, while those from Bohemia typically use red thread. In southern Bohemia, cut fish scales are sometimes sewn onto the skirt and vest for decoration.

Skirt lengths also suggest regional affiliations. In Moravia, skirts are typically worn above the knee, while in Bohemia, they extend below. Vests in Moravia are also cut higher, and sleeves are longer and less puffy. Moravian women also prefer to wear head-scarves, as opposed to their Bohemian counterparts, who favor heavily embroidered caps.

Men's Finery

Kroje for men consist of knee-length trousers, an embroidered, white linen or cotton shirt, and an embroidered vest made of suede, felt, or brocade. Trousers tend to be made of yellow or brown suede or wool in Bohemia and black or dark blue wool with a red or black trimming in Moravia. Although men generally wear thick, knee-high socks and tall leather boots, their hats are clearly distinct. Moravian men wear narrow-brimmed hats decorated with ribbons and feathers, while Bohemian men wear black, large-brimmed hats and neckerchiefs.

Above: **Young men wearing traditional Moravian costumes have long feathers in their hats, which indicate that they are bachelors. Moravian men sometimes wear embroidered boots and thick, richly embroidered belts. The young women, on the other hand, are dressed in full and colorful traditional Moravian skirts. For Moravian women, the patterns on their headscarves and the way they are worn indicate the regions from which the wearers' originate.**

Václav Havel — Playwright to President

Václav Havel, a well-known writer, playwright, and dissident, was the Czech Republic's first president.

From Playwright to Dissident

In 1936, Havel was born in Prague to a family of businessmen and intellectuals. After the 1948 coup in Czechoslovakia, Havel's family became unpopular with the communist government, and young Havel was not allowed to attend high school as a result. Undeterred, Havel later attended night school while working as a laboratory assistant by day. He went on to study economics at the Czech Technical University even though he first applied to study the arts. His first application was rejected because of his family's political reputation.

Havel developed a strong interest in the arts and began writing plays while working as a stagehand. In 1968, the

Above: **Václav Havel was brought up in a family rich in the intellectual tradition, which shaped his thoughts and values.**

Left: **Thousands of Czech students fill Wenceslas Square to support the election of Václav Havel as the country's president. A strong dissident movement led by Havel resulted in the fall of communism in the country.**

Left: Václav Havel waves farewell to the crowd during his final speech as president of the Czech Republic. In February 2003, Havel stepped down from presidency. For having been Czechoslovakia's last president, the Czech Republic's first president, and a strong defender of democracy and human rights throughout his life, Havel earned the love and respect of the Czech people.

communist crackdown ended Havel's artistic freedom. Angered by censorship and persecution, Havel joined other artists and intellectuals in signing a manifesto, called Charter 77, to protest the communist oppression of the Czech people. Although many of his contemporaries were arrested, Havel was unshaken and refused to stop his anticommunist writings. Havel was repeatedly arrested for his views and served five years in prison during the 1970s and 1980s.

From Dissident to President

In November 1989, Havel founded the Civic Forum, which eventually orchestrated the Velvet Revolution. He was elected president of Czechoslovakia in December 1989. In 1992, Havel resigned from the presidency of Czechoslovakia to protest the country's breakup in the Velvet Divorce. However, he agreed the following year to serve as the president of the new Czech Republic. While in office, Havel saw to the development of two new constitutions and facilitated the country's acceptance into NATO. He also helped steer the Czech Republic toward fulfilling the conditions necessary for joining the European Union. Havel has been awarded numerous prestigious international prizes for his literary work and civic activities.

RELATIONS WITH NORTH AMERICA

Millions of North Americans can trace their ancestry back to Bohemia and Moravia. During the Czech Republic's successive periods of occupation, first by the Hapsburgs, then by Nazi Germany, and finally the Soviet Union, a large number of Czechs found themselves in exile. Others left the country to escape economic hardship and political oppression. Many of them sought refuge in Canada and the United States and were granted asylum and citizenship. Over time, Czech communities developed throughout North America. As the number of immigrants increased, their influence increased as well.

Opposite: **Madeleine Albright was the highest ranking female official in U.S. history when she became secretary of state in 1997. She was born in Prague in 1937.**

Today, evidence of Czech culture can be seen throughout North America in the names of cities, buildings, and monuments. Perhaps more important is the fact that many Americans and Canadians of Czech ancestry have influenced the course of North American history, culture, and sports.

Relations between North America and the Czech Republic are firm because of strong historical ties and similar political outlooks. The United States and Canada have played a role in Czech history as countries that have accepted and supported Czech dissidents during times of trouble.

Above: **Czech president Václav Havel (*second from right*) meets with U.S senators on a visit to the United States in 1997. The Czech Senate is modeled after the U.S. Senate.**

History of Relations

The United States and its allies encouraged the formation of the original state of Czechoslovakia in 1918. Tomáš G. Masaryk, who became Czechoslovakia's first president, visited the United States several times and developed close relations with U.S. officials. Masaryk signed the Czechoslovak Declaration of Independence, which was modeled on the U.S. Declaration of Independence. He was a firm advocate of democracy and human rights.

During the Nazi occupation of Czechoslovakia and during World War II, many Czechs fled the country and fought alongside the Allies. In 1942, the United States recognized the government-in-exile led by Edvard Beneš as the legitimate government of Czechoslovakia. Once the war ended, the Beneš government was reinstated, and political and economic ties between the United States and Czechoslovakia resumed.

Relations, however, cooled in 1948 after the Soviet-backed coup in Czechoslovakia. Two months after the coup, the United States implemented the Marshall Plan, which aimed to provide

Left: **President Tomáš Masaryk was elected Czechoslovakia's first president while he was still in the United States.**

Left: Canadian prime minister Jean Chretien (*left*) and Czech president Václav Havel wave to the crowd gathered in front of the Canadian parliament building in Ottowa, Canada. There are Czech communities in Canada today because of Canada's support for Czech dissidents and emigrants in the past.

aid to the countries that had been worst hit during World War II and to promote democracy in those countries. Although Czechoslovakians had expressed interest in signing the Marshall Plan before the coup, the Soviet leadership would not allow the country's participation.

When Soviet troops invaded Czechoslovakia in 1968, relations with the United States soured further. The United States even referred the matter of the Soviet invasion to the United Nations Security Council, but no action was taken. Throughout the period of Soviet "normalization," many exiled Czech dissidents had the support of the United States.

American-Czechoslovak relations improved considerably after the Velvet Revolution in 1989. In 1990, on his first visit to the United States, Czechoslovakia's president, Václav Havel, was well received. During his speech to the U.S. Congress, Havel was interrupted by standing ovations several times.

When the splitting of Czechoslovakia was first proposed, U.S. leaders were concerned that the Velvet Divorce would cause regional unrest and tension. The United States, however, recognized both the Czech Republic and Slovakia as independent nations in 1993 and maintains good relations with both countries.

Canada is also considered a strong ally, having sheltered political refugees and Czech dissidents, especially during the height of the communist oppression.

Left: **U.S. President George W. Bush (***right***) shakes hands with President Václav Havel, who was at the White House in September 2002 to discuss the war on terrorism and the disarmament of Iraq. The Czech Republic supports the United States on both issues, having had a history of good relations with the United States over many years.**

Current Relations

Since the Velvet Revolution and the subsequent split with Slovakia, there has been a considerable improvement in the economic, political, and social ties between the Czech Republic and the United States. The United States has supported the county's membership in a number of international organizations, including NATO and the WTO, and has provided assistance in privatizing and restructuring the postcommunist economy. The United States continues to support the country's economic and political transition.

Canadian support of the Czech Republic is also strong. A technological program between the two countries has brought the Czech Republic some U.S. $20 million in projects since 1993. Trade and investment between North America and the Czech Republic have been increasing. The United States is one the country's top ten trading partners. The Czech North American Chamber of Commerce was set up to facilitate business relations between American and Canadian companies and Czech businesses.

The Czech Republic supports the war on terrorism, and showed some significant support for the United States in the 2003 war in Iraq. The country stationed a chemical and biological weapons detection unit in Kuwait. It is also seeking to be part of an international stabilization force in Iraq and to participate in Iraq's postwar reconstruction.

Early Immigrants

Although there are various reports of Czechs having traveled to the United States as early as the first part of the sixteenth century, the first documented Czech immigrant in the United States was Augustin Hermann, who arrived in 1633 as an employee of the West India Company. Hermann is credited with drawing the first maps of Virginia and Maryland.

In 1735, a group of Hussites, also known as Moravian Brethren, who had been exiled from the Czech lands, made their way to North America. They settled in Georgia, Pennsylvania, Ohio, North Carolina, and, eventually, New York. By the time of the Declaration of Independence in 1776, more than two thousand Moravian Brethren were living in the United States.

Many Czech immigrants arrived in the United States between 1865 and 1914. Economic difficulties drove them to emigrate, and most were farmers or artisans seeking better opportunities. These immigrants established and fostered the close-knit American Czech community that still exists today. Throughout the nineteenth century, schools, societies, and associations were set up to support the growing Czech population. In 1856, the first school teaching the Czech language and history opened in New York.

THE FIRST CZECH IN AMERICA

Despite the many immigrants that preceded him, Czech immigrant Karel Jonáš (1840–1896), also known as Charles Jonas, is referred to as "the First Czech in America" because of his role in both the Czech and American communities. He moved to the United States in 1863 to edit a Czech newspaper. In 1885, he was made the U.S. consul in Prague. In 1890, he was elected the lieutenant-governor of Wisconsin, and in 1894, he was appointed the U.S. consul in St. Petersburg (Russia) and in Crefeld (Germany).

Left: **Scores of Czech immigrants escaping religious and political oppression arrive at U.S. ports in 1921. Most of these immigrants were well educated, and many became successful professionals in the northern cities.**

Setting up Communities

Many Czech immigrants to the United States settled on farms in Nebraska, Texas, Iowa, Minnesota, South Dakota, Kansas, North Dakota, and Oklahoma, or in the mining communities in the Northeast and Midwest. Significant Czech settlements sprung up in Wisconsin, along with the first Czech newspaper that began around 1860 in the city of Racine, Wisconsin. Racine was the first American city with a large number of Czech immigrants.

Czech factory workers, merchants, and professionals also flocked to northern cities, within which ethnic towns were established. Soon, large Czech communities began to develop in the cities of Baltimore, Maryland; Chicago, Illinois; Cleveland, Ohio; Milwaukee, Wisconsin; Minneapolis, Minnesota; Omaha, Nebraska; St. Louis, Missouri; and New York City. Other Czech immigrants settled in La Grange, Texas and Cedar Rapids, Iowa.

Political Refugees

Prior to World War II, the Czech population in the United States swelled with the arrival of political refugees fleeing Nazi-occupied Czechoslovakia. In 1942, a town in the state

Left: Anton Cermak (*middle*) visited London in 1932, a year after being elected mayor of Chicago.

Left: The National Czech and Slovak Museum and Library in Cedar Rapids, Iowa, offers programs and activities that enable people to learn more about the Czech culture and language.

of Illinois was renamed "Lidice" to commemorate the village in central Bohemia that was destroyed by Nazi soldiers.

Another wave of emigration to the United States and Canada occurred in the wake of the communist coup and the Soviet invasion of 1968. Former members of the Czechoslovak parliament who had sought refuge in the United States formed the Council for Free Czechoslovakia in Washington, D.C. Throughout the Soviet occupation, the United States became home to many Czech dissidents and refugees, particularly those who had access to the country through sports or the arts.

Immigration Today

The pace of Czech immigration to the United States has slowed since the Velvet Revolution and the subsequent independence of the Czech Republic. At the same time, there has been a reawakening in some American Czechs of pride in their heritage. According to the 2000 U.S. census, some 1.7 million Americans claimed to be of Czech or Czechoslovakian descent. Texas has the largest number of people who claim Czech or Czechoslovakian ancestry. Czech organizations set up in different states provide a place where members of the U.S. Czech community can socialize and learn about their culture and roots.

CZECH IMMIGRANTS IN CANADA

The early Czech immigrants to Canada formed small farming communities in the prairies of southeastern Saskatchawan. After World War I, immigrants began to settle in cities such as Winnipeg, Toronto, and Montreal, where they established factories and businesses. One such Czech is Thomas J. Bata, who moved his shoe business from Moravia to Toronto when the Nazis occupied Czechoslovakia. Today, Canadians of Czech and Slovak descent can be found in Canadian arts, politics, sports, and media.

Left: **Prague is the headquarters (*right*) of Radio Free Europe, an organization financed by the United States government that provided news and information to the Czech people while they were under communist censorship in Czechoslovakia. It is still in operation today, broadcasting programs and commentaries for a world audience.**

Americans in the Czech Republic

Since the 1989 Velvet Revolution, many Czech Americans have returned to the Czech Republic to rediscover their ancestry. Some Americans have chosen to study in the country, taking some of the many English-language courses offered at Czech universities. A number of students take advantage of exchange programs between the Czech Republic and Canada and the United States. Others choose to work in the country as teachers or college professors, while yet others have set up businesses in the country. In Prague, international schools cater to expatriate families with children.

Prague is also a magnet for American writers and poets, many of whom have spent considerable periods of time there. One such American is Alan Levy, the famous author and journalist and founding editor-in-chief of the *Prague Post*, the city's largest English-language newspaper. Levy was born in New York City in 1932. He and his family moved to Prague in 1967. During the Soviet occupation, Levy repeatedly criticized the communist regime. He was expelled from Czechoslovakia in 1971 and wrote *Rowboat to Prague,* a book credited with heightening Western awareness of the plight of Czechoslovakia, in 1972. After the Velvet Revolution, Levy returned to Prague, where he still lives today.

Famous Czech Americans

There is no short list of the number of Czechs or Americans of Czech descent that have made their mark on American science, art, politics, sports, and culture. Starting as early as the nineteenth century, Czech Frederick George Novy pioneered the study of bacteriology in the United States. Eugene Cernan was the commander of Apollo 17, which landed on the moon in 1972. Cernan was born in Chicago to Czechoslovak parents.

Andy Warhol, the renowned pop art personality, was the son of Czechoslovak immigrants. He changed his last name from Warhola to Warhol. Oscar-winning film director Miloš Forman was born in a small town near Prague and now lives in the United States. In the area of sports, tennis superstars Ivan Lendl and Martina Navrátilová were both born in the Czech Republic. Navrátilová sought political asylum in the United States in 1975 and lives in Aspen, Colorado today. Lendl moved to the United States in 1986 and now lives in Greenwich, Connecticut.

In addition to those who became Americans, many famous Czech personalities spent considerable time in the United States. They include Czechoslovakian president Tomáš G. Masaryk, composer Antonín Dvořák, and artist Alphonse Mucha. Two of the greatest stars in NHL ice hockey, Jaromír Jágr and Dominik Hašek, are Czech but currently reside in the United States.

OTTO WICHTERLE (1913–1998)

Millions of Americans today use soft contact lenses. The inventor of the soft contact lens was Otto Wichterle, a Czech born in Moravia.

Left: Ivana Trump (*left*) — Czechoslovak skier, former wife of tycoon Donald Trump, and model — was born in the Czech town of Zlín.

83

Cultural Influences

When Czechs immigrated to the United States, they usually remained close-knit and lived in settlements among themselves. These early settlements bore Czech names, and, while some were eventually absorbed into larger towns and cities, a great deal have kept their original names. For example, Pilsen in Chicago is named after Plzeň in Bohemia.

In addition to retaining their names, these communities have done much to preserve and honor their heritage. Regular community festivals that include traditional Czech folk dancing and music are held throughout the year. Sometimes, traditional costumes are worn for these occasions.

Texas Czechs

Texas has a large and thriving Czech community. Over the years, a unique form of folk music, known as "Texas Czech" music, has developed. This musical style is a combination of the folk melodies played by early Czech settlers in Texas with other European elements, such as brass bands and accordions, and American Western Swing music. The result is uniquely Texan Czech. The National Polka Festival, which celebrates the Bohemian dance, is held in Ennis, Texas, each year.

Czech Cultural Ties

Interactive learning centers, Czech museums, and Czech heritage societies enable young Czech Americans to learn about their Czech ancestors. Some attend summer camps to learn the Czech language. The American Friends of the Czech Republic is an organization that aims at educating leaders and policy makers in the United States. This organization has hosted Czech dignitaries, coordinated important Czech events in the United States, facilitated contact between U.S. and Czech diplomats, and, in 2002, set up a flood relief fund to help Czech flood victims.

The Czech Center in New York organizes cultural programs to increase American awareness of Czech culture. It also serves as a resource center for students and business people interested in the Czech Republic. The Czechoslovak Society of Arts and Sciences (SVU) is also a widely-known organization, started by Czechoslovak intellectuals in 1958. It is now a forum for Czech professionals.

AMERICAN SOKOL

Sokol, the Czech sporting organization started to promote Czech culture and exercise, enjoys a following in the United States. In 2000, there were approximately forty-three American Sokol clubs, with a total of about 10,000 members.

Opposite: **A group of sculptors in the 1930s work on monuments, such as this statue of Tomáš G. Masaryk. In September 2002, a similar statue of Masaryk, created in 1937 and hidden in the National Gallery of Prague during the Nazi invasion of Czechoslovakia, was placed in the new T.G. Masaryk Park in Washington, D.C. The statue was a gift to the United States from the Czech Republic. The dedication ceremony, which was attended by representatives from the Czech, Slovak, and U.S. governments, concluded with a dinner hosted by the American Friends of the Czech Republic.**

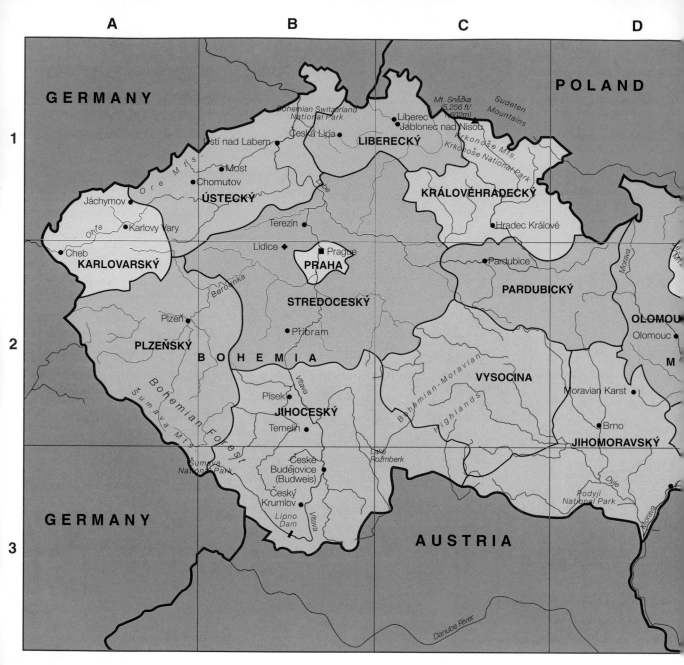

A   B   C   D

GERMANY

POLAND

1

Bohemian Switzerland
National Park

Liberec

Mt. Sněžka
(5,256 ft/
1,602m)

Sudeten
Mountains

Jablonec nad Nisou

Ústí nad Labem

Česká Lípa

LIBERECKÝ

Krkonoše Mts.

Krkonoše National Park

Most

Labe

Chomutov

ÚSTECKÝ

KRÁLOVÉHRADECKÝ

Ore Mts.

Jáchymov

Terezín

Hradec Králové

Karlovy Vary

Ohře

Cheb

Lidice

Prague

KARLOVARSKÝ

PRAHA

Pardubice

PARDUBICKÝ

OLOMOU

Berounka

STREDOCESKÝ

2

Plzeň

Příbram

Olomouc

PLZEŇSKÝ

B O H E M I A

M

Vltava

Bohemian-Moravian

VYSOCINA

Moravian Karst

Morava

Bohemian Forest

Písek

Highlands

Šumava Mts.

JIHOCESKÝ

Brno

Temelín

Lake
Rožmberk

JIHOMORAVSKÝ

Šumava
National Park

České
Budějovice
(Budweis)

Český
Krumlov

Podyjí
National Park

Dyje

GERMANY

Lipno
Dam

Vltava

AUSTRIA

Morava

3

Danube River

Austria A3–D3

Berounka River B2
Bohemia A1–B3
Bohemian Forest A2–B3
Bohemian-Moravian
   Highlands C2
Bohemian Switzerland
   National Park B1
Brno D2

Česká Lípa B1
České Budějovice
   (Budweis) B3

Český Krumlov B3
Cheb A2

Dyje River D3

Germany A1–A3

Hodonín D3
Hradec Králové C1

Jablonec nad Nisou C1
Jáchymov A1
Javorníky Mountains E2

Jeseníky Mountains
   D1–D2
Jihoceský (region)
   B2–B3
Jihomoravský (region)
   D2–D3

Karlovarský (region)
   A1-A2
Karlovy Vary A1
Královehradecký
   (region) C1–D1
Krkonoše Mountains C1

Krkonoše National
   Park C1

Labe River B1–C2
Liberec C1
Liberecký (region)
   B1–C1
Lidice B2
Lipno Dam B3
Little Carpathian
   Mountains E2–E3

Morava River D1–D3

———	International Boundary
———	Regional Boundary
■	Capital
●	City
▲	Highest Point
◆	Historical Site
～～	River

Above: Tourists stop for a rest at a statue along Charles Bridge in Prague.

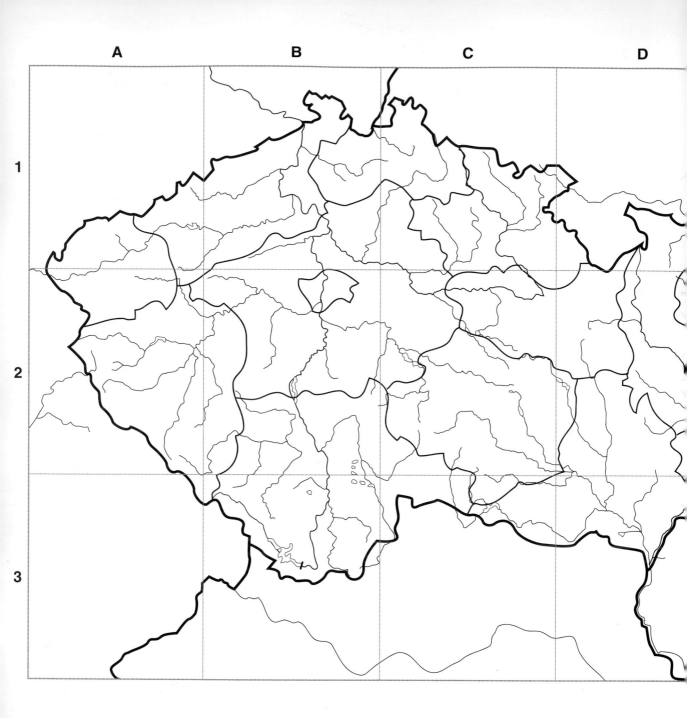

A   B   C   D

1

2

3

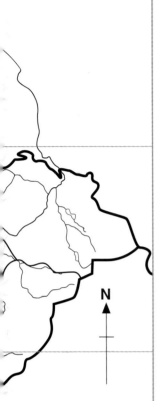

How Is Your Geography?

Learning to identify the main geographical areas and points of a country can be challenging. Although it may seem difficult at first to memorize the locations and spellings of major cities or the names of mountain ranges, rivers, deserts, lakes, and other prominent physical features, the end result of this effort can be very rewarding. Places you previously did not know existed will suddenly come to life when referred to in world news, whether in newspapers, television reports, other books and reference sources, or on the Internet. This knowledge will make you feel a bit closer to the rest of the world, with its fascinating variety of cultures and physical geography.

This map can be duplicated for use in a classroom. (PLEASE DO NOT WRITE IN THIS BOOK!) Students can then fill in any requested information on their individual map copies. The student can also make a copy of the map and use it as a study tool to practice identifying place names and geographical features on his or her own.

Above: **The design of this castle in Moravia includes elements of the Baroque style of architecture.**

Czech Republic at a Glance

Official Name   Czech Republic (Ceská Republika)

Capital   Prague (Praha)

Official Language   Czech

Population   10.3 million (July 2002 estimate)

Land Area   30,400 square miles (78,740 square km)

Administrative Divisions   13 regions (kraje) and 1 capital city: Jihoceský, Jihomoravský, Karlovarsky, Královéhradecký, Liberecký, Moravskoslezský, Olomoucký, Pardubický, Plzeňský, Stredoceský, Ústecký, Vysocina, Zlinský, and Prague (Praha).

Highest Point   Mount Sněžka at 5,256 feet (1,602 m)

Major Rivers   Vltava River, Labe (Elbe) River, Odra (Oder) River, and the Morava River

Religions   Roman Catholic (39.2 percent), Protestant (4.6 percent), Orthodox (3 percent), other (13.4 percent) [atheist (39.8 percent)]

Ethnic Groups   Bohemian (81.2 percent), Moravian (13.2 percent), Slovak (3.1 percent), Polish (0.6 percent), German (0.5 percent), Silesian (0.4 percent), Roma (0.3 percent), Hungarian (0.2 percent)

Holidays   St. Wenceslas Day (September 28), Czech Founding Day (October 28), Christmas (December 24-26)

Major Imports   Machinery and transport equipment, raw materials, chemicals.

Major Trade Partners Germany, Slovakia, UK, Austria, Poland

Currency   Czech crown (Ceská koruna – CZK). (29.707 CZK = U.S. $1 as of 2003)

Opposite: **The Valdstejn Palace is located in Malá Strana, a district of Prague.**

Glossary

Czech Vocabulary

babička (BAHB-ish-ka): grandmother.

chalupa (KHAH-lu-pah): country cottages made of wood.

chata (KHAH-tah): country chalets.

hospoda (HO-spo-dah): drinking hall.

houby (HO-bay): wild mushrooms.

kraslice (KRAH-slih-zee): decorated eggs.

kraje (KHRA-ay): regions.

kroje (KRO-yih): traditional Czech folk costumes.

mariáš (MA-ree-ahsh): Czech card game, similar to the game of rummy.

pivo (PEE-vo): Czech beer.

pomlázka (PO-mlah-skah): braided willow branches tied together to form a switch.

Sokol (SOH-kohl): a Czech exercise organization that promotes national fitness and health.

Svícková (SVEETCH-ko-vah): Sliced beef sirloin.

Veprŏ-knedlo-zelo (vepro-KNED-loh-ZEE-loh): roast pork served with dumplings and sauerkraut.

Vysvĕdčeni (VEES-vehd-cheh-nee): basic school diploma.

English Vocabulary

accession: the act by which one nation becomes party to an agreement already in force between other powers.

Allied forces: an association of countries, consisting of mainly of Great Britain, the Soviet Union, and the United States, that opposed the Axis (Germany, Italy, and Japan) powers in World War II.

anthracite: a hard coal that, when burned, gives off heat but little smoke.

Art Nouveau: international style of decoration and architecture that developed in the 1880s and 1890s.

autonomy: power of self-government.

betrothed: promised for marriage.

brocade: a rich silk fabric with raised patterns, sometimes in gold and silver.

calisthenics: slow, rhythmic exercises.

canonized: declared officially as a saint.

catholicizing: converting people to the Roman Catholic faith.

constitution: a document defining the fundamental laws of a country.

coup d'état: sudden overthrow of a government, usually by a small group that replaces the top power figures.

decathlete: an athlete that competes in a decathlon, a 10-event athletic contest.

deforestation: the cutting down of large areas of forests, usually for industrial or agricultural purposes.

diacritical marks: marks placed over or attached to letters to indicate special pronunciations or stresses.

dissident: a person who disagrees with an established political system.

egalitarian: supportive of human equality especially with respect to social, political, and economic rights and privileges.

exemplified: used as an example.

extermination: the killing off all individuals in a group.

facet: a small, flat surface cut into an object, such as a piece of crystal.

fauna: animal life.

flora: plant life.

foundries: places where glass or metal is cast and molded.

frescoes: paintings done on wet plaster.

grotesque: characterized by a strange or eccentric appearance.

heresy: the opposition to and rejection of official doctrine of a church.

Holocaust: the systematic destruction of European Jews by the Nazis before and during World War II.

Hussites: followers of the religious reforms of Jan Hus.

infamous: having a bad reputation.

manifesto: a public declaration of motives or intentions by a group or person.

marionettes: puppets operated from above using strings.

morello: any of several varieties of sour cherry with dark red skin and red juice.

opponents: people who are against another; enemies.

oppression: unjust or cruel exercise of authority or power.

Order of Poor Clares: order of Franciscan nuns started by St. Clare of Assisi.

parliamentary democracy: political system whereby democratically elected representatives make decisions on behalf of the public.

photosynthesis: the process by which plants convert sunlight into energy.

pogrom: an organized massacre of a group of helpless people, such as the Nazi attacks on European Jews.

polka: a Bohemian dance tune in 2/4 time.

Prague Spring: name given to the period in 1968 when Czechoslovakia was under the control of reformist communist leader, Alexander Dubček.

privatization: selling previously state-owned organizations to the private sector to operate and own.

prolific: fruitful; abundant

propaganda: ideas or doctrines spread systematically to lead people into believing one's cause or agenda.

Renaissance: the great period of revival of art, literature, and learning in Europe from the fourteenth to sixteenth centuries that began in Italy and spread to other countries and marked the transition from the medieval world to the modern.

sanatoriums: establishments for the treatment of ill patients.

satires: literary works meant to ridicule human vice or follies.

socialism: a political and economic system advocating collective ownership of the means of production and distribution of goods.

sovereignty: supreme power; freedom from external control.

Tennis Grand Slam: the achievement of winning the four major tennis championships: Australian Open, French Open, Wimbledon, and U.S. Open, in the same calendar year.

tobogganing: moving rapidly down a mountain slope on a narrow, flat sled made of thin boards curved back at one end.

Velvet Divorce: the separation in 1993 of the former Czechoslovakia into the Czech Republic and Slovakia.

Velvet Revolution: the peaceful ousting of the Soviet leadership from Czechoslovakia in 1989.

More Books to Read

Baubles, Buttons and Beads: The Heritage of Bohemia. Sibylle Jargstorf (Schiffer)

Czech Republic. Cultures of the World series. Efstathia Sioras (Marshall Cavendish)

Czech Republic. Country Insights, City, and Village Life series. Rob Humphreys (Raintree/ Steck-Vaughn)

Czech Republic. Modern Nations of the World series. Petra Press (Lucent)

Czech Republic in Pictures. Visual Geography series. Stacy Taus-Bolstad, Alison Behnke (Lerner)

Dominik Hasek. Hockey Heroes series. Sean Rossiter (Greystone)

Favorite Fairy Tales Told in Czechoslovakia. Virginia Haviland (Beech Tree)

Fireflies in the Dark: The Story of Friedl Dicker-Brandeis and the Children of Terezin. Susan Goldman Rubin (Holiday House)

Hana's Suitcase. Karen Levine (Alvert Whitman & Co.)

I Never Saw Another Butterfly: Children's Drawings and Poems from Terezin Concentration Camp 1942-1944. Hana Volavková, editor (Schocken Books)

Václav Havel and the Velvet Revolution. People in Focus series. Jeffrey Symynkywicz (Dillon Press)

Videos

Globe Trekker: Czech Republic and Slovakia. (555 Productions)

Prague. Super Cities series. (Questar)

Web Sites

www.cia.gov/cia/publications/factbook/geos/ez.html

www.czech.cz

www.mzv.cz/washington/

Due to the dynamic nature of the Internet, some web sites stay current longer than others. To find additional web sites, use a reliable search engine with one or more of the following keywords to help you locate information about Czech Republic. Keywords: *Bohemian Kingdom, Czechoslovakia, Havel, Velvet Revolution, Prague, and World Heritage list.*

Index